PAPER BACK LYRICS

COMPLETE LYRICS FOR OVER 200 SONGS

The

1950s

HAL•LEONARD®

ISBN-13: 978-1-4234-1192-5
ISBN-10: 1-4234-1192-7

HAL•LEONARD®
CORPORATION
7777 W. BLUEMOUND RD. P.O. BOX 13819 MILWAUKEE, WI 53213

Visit Hal Leonard Online at
www.halleonard.com

CONTENTS

The ABC's of Love

Words and Music by Richard Barrett and Morris Levy

recorded by Frankie Lymon & The Teenagers

Du bop shu-boom,
Bom bom bom bom bom.
Du bop shu-boom,
Bom bom bom bom bom.

I'll always want you,
Because my heart is true.
Come, come, come closer
And I'll tell you of the ABC's.

Darling, believe me,
Ev'ry day my love grows strong.
Find a place there in your heart
And I'll tell you of the ABC's.

Gosh knows I love you,
Heaven knows it's true.
I want to be near you,
J, K, L, M, N, O, P, Q.

Run, honey, and don't be blind.
Sugar, you stay on my mind.
True love is hard to find,
I'll tell you of the ABC's.

You made me love you.
Vow always to be true.
W, X, Y, and Z.
I've told you of the ABC's.

Run, honey, and don't be blind.
Sugar, you stay on my mind.
True love is hard to find,
I'll tell you of the ABC's.

You made me love you.
Vow always to be true.
W, X, Y, and Z.
I've told you of the ABC's.
Told you of the ABC's.

All I Have to Do Is Dream

Words and Music by Boudleaux Bryant

recorded by The Everly Brothers

Dream, dream, dream, dream.
Dream, dream, dream, dream.

When I want you in my arms,
When I want you and all your charms,
Whenever I want you,
All I have to do is dream,
Dream, dream, dream.

When I feel blue in the night,
And I need you to hold me tight,
Whenever I want you,
All I have to do is dream.

Bridge:
I can make you mine,
Taste your lips of wine,
Anytime, night or day.
Only trouble is, gee whiz,
I'm dreaming my life away.
I need you so that I could die,
I love you so
And that is why
Whenever I want you
All I have to do is dream.

Repeat Bridge and Last Verse

Dream, dream, dream.
Dream, dream, dream, dream.
Dream.

All Shook Up

Words and Music by Otis Blackwell and Elvis Presley

recorded by Elvis Presley

A-well-a bless my soul, what's wrong with me?
I'm itching like a man on a fuzzy tree.
My friends say I'm actin' queer as a bug.

Refrain:
I'm in love.
I'm all shook up!
Mm, mm, oh, oh, yeah!

My hands are shaky and my knees are weak
I can't seem to stand on my own two feet.
Who do you thank when you have such luck?

Please don't ask what's on my mind,
I'm a little mixed up but I feelin' fine.
When I'm near that girl that I love the best,
My heart beats so it scares me to death!
She touched my hand,
What a chill I got,
Her kisses are like a volcano that's hot!
I'm proud to say she's my buttercup,

Refrain

My tongue gets tied when I try to speak,
My insides shake like a leaf on a tree,
There's only one cure for this soul of mine,
That's to have the girl that I love so fine!
She touched my hand,
What a chill I got,
Her kisses are like a volcano that's hot!
I'm proud to say she's my buttercup,

Refrain Three Times

I'm all shook up! All shook up!

Are You Sincere

Words and Music by Wayne Walker and Lucky Moeller

recorded by Andy Williams

Are you sincere when you say, "I love you?"
Are you sincere when you say "I'll be true?"
Do you mean ev'ry word that my ears have heard?
I'd like to know which way to go,
Will our love grow, are you sincere?

Are you sincere when you say you miss me?
Are you sincere ev'ry time you kiss me?
And are you really mine ev'ry day, all the time?
I'd like to know which way to go,

Will our love grow? Are you sincere?

At the Hop

Words and Music by Arthur Singer, John Madara and David White

recorded by Danny & The Juniors

Ba ba ba ba,
Ba ba ba ba,
Ba ba ba ba,
Ba ba ba ba,
At the hop.

Well, you can rock it, you can roll it,
Do the stomp and even stroll it at the hop.
When the records start a-spinnin'
You calypso and you chicken at the hop.
Do the dance sensations that are sweepin' the nation at the hop.

Refrain:
Let's go to the hop!
Let's go to the hop!
(Oh, baby) Let's go to the hop!
(Oh, baby) Let's go to the hop!
Come on, let's go to the hop!

Well, you can swing it, you can groove it,
You can really start to move it at the hop.
Where the jockey is the smoothest
And the music is the coolest at the hop.
All the cats and the chicks can get their kicks at the hop.

Refrain

Band of Gold

Words and Music by Edythe Wayne and Ronald Dunbar

recorded by Don Cherry, Kit Carson

Now that you're gone all that's left is a band of gold.
All that's left of the dreams I hold is a band of gold
And the memories of what love could be,
If you were still here with me.

You took me from the shelter of a lover
I have never known or loved any other.
We kissed after taking vows but that night on our honeymoon
We stayed in separate rooms.

I prayed in the darkness of one lonely room
Filled with sadness, filled with gloom,
Hoping soon that you'd walk back through that door
And love me like you tried before.

Since you've been gone all that's left is a band of gold,
All that's left of the dreams I hold is a band of gold
And the dream of what love could be
If you were still here with me.

Be-Bop-A-Lula

Words and Music by Tex Davis and Gene Vincent

recorded by Gene Vincent

Be-bop-a-lula, she's my baby.
Be-bop-a-lula, I don't mean maybe.

Refrain:
Be-bop-a-lula, she's my baby.
Be-bop-a-lula, I don't mean maybe.
Be-bop-a-lula, she's my baby doll,
My baby doll, my baby doll.

She's the gal in the red blue jeans.
She's the queen of all the teens.
She's the one that I know.
She's the one that loves me so.

Refrain

She's the one that's got that beat.
She's the one with the flyin' feet.
She's the one that walks around the store.
She's the one that gets more and more.

Refrain

Beep Beep

Words and Music by Carl Ciccetti and Donald Claps

recorded by The Playmates

While riding in my Cadillac, what, to my surprise,
A little Nash Rambler was following me, about one-third my size.
The guy must have wanted it to pass me up
As he kept on tooting his horn. Beep! Beep!
I'll show him that a Cadillac is not a car to scorn.

Refrain:
Beep, beep. (Beep, beep.)
Beep, beep. (Beep, beep.)
His horn went, beep, beep, beep.

(Beep! Beep!).
I pushed my foot down to the floor to give the guy the shake,
But the little Nash Rambler stayed right behind;
   he still had on his brake.
He must have thought his car had more guts
As he kept on tooting his horn. Beep! Beep!
I'll show him that a Cadillac is not a car to scorn.

Refrain

My car went into passing gear and we took off with dust.
And soon we were doin' ninety, must have left him in the dust.
When I peeked in the mirror of my car,
I couldn't believe my eyes.
The little Nash Rambler was right behind, you'd think that guy could fly.

Refrain

Now we're doing a hundred and ten, it certainly was a race.
For a Rambler to pass a Caddy would be a big disgrace.
For the guy who wanted to pass me,
He kept on tooting his horn. Beep! Beep!
I'll show him that a Cadillac is not a car to scorn.

Refrain

Now we're doing a hundred and twenty, as fast as I could go.
The Rambler pulled alongside of me as if I were going slow.
The fellow rolled down his window and yelled for me to hear,
"Hey, buddy, how can I get this car out of second gear?"

Believe What You Say

Words and Music by Dorsey Burnette and Johnny Burnette

recorded by Ricky Nelson

I believe what you say when you say you're goin' steady
With nobody else but me.
I believe what you say when you say ya don't kiss
Nobody else but me.

Refrain:
I believe, do believe,
I believe, yeah believe, pretty baby,
Believe you're goin' steady
With nobody else but me.

Well, there's a-one thing baby, that I want you to know
When you rockin' with me you don't rock too slow.
A-move on in get toe to toe
We're gonna rock 'til we can't rock no more.

Refrain

I believe what you say when you say you don't miss
Nobody else by me.
I believe what you say when you say ya don't kiss
Nobody else but me.

Refrain

Well, when you kiss me baby, then you roll your eyes
I get a funny feelin' that I'm hypnotized.
The chills run all up and down my spine
A-tellin' ev'rybody that you're mine all mine.

Refrain

Oh, yeah well, I believe do believe
I believe, well believe, pretty baby,
Believe you're goin' steady with nobody else but me.

Bibbidi-Bobbidi-Boo
(The Magic Song)

Words by Jerry Livingston
Music by Mack David and Al Hoffman

from Walt Disney's *Cinderella*

Salagadoola menchicka boola
Bibbidi-bobbidi-boo
Put them together and what have you got?
Bibbidi-bobbidi-boo.

Salagadoola menchicka boola
Bibbidi-bobbidi-boo.
It'll do magic, believe it or not,
Bibbidi-bobbidi-boo.

Salagadoola means menchicka booleroo,
But the thing-a-ma-bob that does the job
Is bibbidi-bobbidi-boo.

Salagadoola menchicka boola
Bibbidi-bobbidi-boo.
Put them together and what have you got?
Bibbidi-bobbidi-boo
Bibbidi-bobbidi-boo
Bibbidi-bobbidi-boo.

The Big Hurt

Words and Music by Wayne Shanklin

recorded by Miss Toni Fisher

Now it begins now that you're gone,
Needles and pins twilight till dawn.
Watching that clock till you return,
Lighting that torch and watching it burn.

Now it begins day after day.
This is my life ticking away.
Waiting to hear footsteps that say
Love will appear and this time to stay.

Oh, each time you go I try to pretend.
It's over at last, this time the big hurt will end.
Now it begins now that you're gone,
Needles and pins twilight till dawn.

But if you don't come back again,
I wonder when, oh, when will it end the big hurt.

Black Denim Trousers and Motorcycle Boots

Words and Music by Jerry Leiber and Mike Stoller

recorded by The Cheers

Refrain:
He wore black denim trousers and motorcycle boots
And a black leather jacket with an eagle on the back.
He had a hopped-up cycle that took off like a gun.
That fool was the terror of Highway 101.

Well, he never washed his face and he never combed his hair.
He had axle grease embedded underneath his fingernails.
On the muscle of his arm was a red tattoo,
A picture of a heart saying, "Mother, I love you."

He had a pretty girlfriend by the name of Mary Lou,
But he treated her just like he treated all the rest.
And ev'rybody pitied her 'cause ev'rybody knew
He loved that doggone motorcycle best.

Refrain

Mary Lou, poor girl, she pleaded and she begged him not to leave.
She said, "I've got a feeling if you ride tonight I'll grieve."
But her tears were shed in vain, and her ev'ry word was lost
In the rumble of his engine and the smoke from his exhaust.

He took off like a devil, there was fire in his eyes.
He said, "I'll go a thousand miles before the sun can rise."
But he hit a screaming diesel that was California bound,
And when they cleared the wreckage, all they found

Was his black denim trousers and motorcycle boots
And a black leather jacket with an eagle on the back.
But they couldn't find the cycle that took off like a gun,
And they never found the terror of Highway 101.

Blue Hawaii

Words and Music by Leo Robin and Ralph Rainger

recorded by Billy Vaughn

Night and you and blue Hawaii,
The night is heavenly,
And you are heaven to me.
Lovely you and blue Hawaii,
With all this loveliness there should be love.

Come with me while the moon is on the sea.
The night is young and so are we.
Dreams come true in blue Hawaii
And mine could all come true
This magic night of nights with you.

Blue Suede Shoes

Words and Music by Carl Lee Perkins

recorded by Carl Perkins, Elvis Presley

Well it's one for the money, two for the show,
Three to get ready, now go, cat, go, but

Refrain:
Don't you step on my blue suede shoes.
You can do anything but lay off of my blue suede shoes.

Well, you can knock me down, step on my face,
Slander my name all over the place;
Do anything that you want to do,
But uh-uh, honey, lay off of my shoes.

Refrain

Well, you can burn my house, steal my car,
Drink my cider from an old fruit jar;
Do anything that you want to do,
But uh-uh, honey, lay off of my shoes.

Refrain

Blueberry Hill

Words and Music by Al Lewis, Larry Stock and Vincent Rose

recorded by Fats Domino

I found my thrill on Blueberry Hill,
On Blueberry Hill when I found you.
The moon stood still on Blueberry Hill
And lingered until my dreams came true.

The wind in the willow played love's sweet melody;
But all of those vows we made were never meant to be.
Though we're apart, you're part of me still,
For you were my thrill on Blueberry Hill.

Born to Be with You

Words and Music by Don Robertson

recorded by the Chordettes

By your side, satisfied through and through
'Cause I was born to be with you.

Refrain:
Hum, hum,
Hum, hum, hum.

Wondrously, love can see;
So I knew that I was born to be with you.

Refrain

Do I find peace of mind? Yes, I do!
'Cause I was born to be with you.

Refrain

Hum, hum.

Book of Love

Words and Music by Warren Davis, George Malone and Charles Patrick

recorded by The Monotones

Tell me, tell me, tell me,
Oh, who wrote the book of love?
I've got to know the answer;
Was it someone from above?

Refrain:
I wonder, wonder who, who,
Who wrote the book of love?

I love you, darling,
Baby, you know I do.
I've got to see this book of love,
Find out why it's true.

Refrain

Chapter one says to love her,
To love her with all your heart.
Chapter two you tell her
You're never, never, never, never ever gonna part.
In chapter three remember
The meaning of romance.
In chapter four you break up,
But you give her just one more chance.

Refrain

Baby, baby, baby,
I love you, yes, I do.
Well, it says so in this book of love,
Ours is the one that's true.

Refrain

Botch-A-Me
(Ba-ba-baciami piccina)

English lyric and music adapted by Eddie Y. Stanley
Italian words and music by R. Morbelli and L. Astore

recorded by Rosemary Clooney

Botch-a-me, I'll botch-a-you and ev'ry thing goes crazy!

Bah, bah, botch-a-me, bambino, bah-bah bo, bo
Boca piccolino, when-a you kiss me and I'm a-kiss-a you,
Tra la la la la la la la loo.

Bah, bah, botch-a-me, my baby, bah-bah bo, bo,
Just say "yes" and maybe if-a you squeeze me and
   I'm a-squeeze-a you,
Tra la la la la la la la loo.

Bee-o, bye-oh, bee-oo boo,
Won't you botch-a botch-a me?
Bee-oo, bye-oh, bee-oo, boo,

When you botch-a-me I botch-a-you, and ev'rything goes crazy.

Bah, bah, botch-a-me, bambino, bah-bah bo, bo,
Boca piccolino and then we will raise a great big family,
Tra la la la la la la la lee.

Bah, bah, botch-a-me, my baby, bah-bah bo, bo,
Just say "yes" and maybe if-a you squeeze me and
    I'm a-squeeze-a you,
Tra la la la la la la la loo.

Bee-oo, bye-oh, bee-oo boo,
Won't you botch-a botch-a me?
Spoken: Kiss me.
Bee-oo, bye-oh, bee-oo, boo,
When you botcha-me I botch-a-you,
Spoken: Come on-a-you kiss-a-me, eh?

Bah, bah, botch-a-me, bambino, bah-bah bo, bo,
Boca piccolino and then we will raise a great big family,
Tra la la la la la la la

Bee-oo, bye-oh, bee-oo boo,
Botch-a-me, bambino, botch-a-me.
Spoken: That's nice!

A Boy Without a Girl

Words and Music by Sidney Jacobson and Ruth Sexter

recorded by Frankie Avalon

A boy without a girl
Is a song without a tune,
Is a year without a June, my love.
A boy without a girl
Is a day without a night,
Is a star without a light, my love.

And since you've come to me,
All the world has come to shine,
'Cause I've found girl who's really mine.
And if you stay with me,
All your life you'll never be
A girl without a boy, my love.

Butterfly

Words and Music by Kal Mann and Bernie Lowe

recorded by Charlie Gracie, Andy Williams

You tell me you love me, you say you'll be true,
Then you fly around with somebody new,
But I'm crazy about you, you butterfly.

You're treatin' me mean, you're makin' me cry.
I've made up my mind to tell you goodbye,
But I'm no good without you, you butterfly.

I knew from the first time I kissed you
That you were the troublin' kind,
'Cause the honey drips from your sweet lips;
One taste and I'm out of my mind.

I love you so much, I know what I'll do,
I'm clippin your wings; your flyin' is through,
'Cause I'm crazy about you, you butterfly.

Bye Bye Love

Words and Music by Felice Bryant and Boudleaux Bryant

recorded by The Everly Brothers

There goes my baby
With someone new.
She sure looks happy;
I sure am blue.
She was my baby
Till he stepped in.
Good-bye to romance
That might have been.

Refrain:
Bye bye, love.
Bye bye, happiness.
Hello loneliness.
I think I'm gonna cry.
Bye bye, love.
Bye bye, sweet caress.
Hello emptiness.
I feel like I could die.
Bye bye, my love, good-bye.

I'm through with romance,
I'm through with love.
I'm through with counting
The stars above.
And here's the reason
That I'm so free,
My loving baby
Is through with me.

Refrain

Canadian Sunset

Words by Norman Gimbel
Music by Eddie Heywood

recorded by Hugo Winterhalter/Eddie Heywood, Andy Williams

Once, I was alone.
So lonely, and then you came,
Out of the nowhere,
Like the sun up from the hills.

Cold, cold was the wind.
Warm, warm were your lips,
Out there on that ski trail,
Where your kiss filled me with thrills.

A weekend in Canada,
A change of scene was the most I bargained for.
And then I discovered you, and in your eyes I found
A love that I couldn't ignore.

Down came the sun.
Fast, fast beat my heart.
I knew, as the sun set,
From that day we'd never part.

Chances Are

Words by Al Stillman
Music by Robert Allen

recorded by Johnny Mathis

Chances are 'cause I wear a silly grin,
The moment you come into view,
Chances are you think that I'm in love with you.

Just because my composure sort of slips,
The moment that your lips meet mine,
Chances are you think my heart's your valentine.

In the magic of moonlight,
When I sigh, "Hold me close, dear,"
Chances are you believe the stars
That fill the skies, are in my eyes.

Guess you feel you'll always be
The one and only one for me.
And if you think you could,
Well, chances are your chances are awf'ly good.

Changing Partners

Words by Joe Darion
Music by Larry Coleman

recorded by Patti Page

We were waltzin' together
To a dreamy melody,
When they called out change partners
And you waltzed away from me.
Now my arms feel so empty
As I gaze around the floor.
And I'll keep on changing partners
Till I hold you once more.

Though we danced for one moment,
And too soon we had to part,
In that wonderful moment,
Something happened to my heart.
So, I'll keep changing partners
Till you're in my arms again.
Oh, my darlin',
I will never change partners again.

Chantilly Lace

Words and Music by J.P. Richardson

recorded by Big Bopper

Chantilly lace
And a pretty face
And a pony tail
Hangin' down,
Wiggle in her walk
And a giggle in her talk,
Makes the world go 'round.

Ain't nothin' in this world
Like a big-eyed girl
To make me act so funny,
Make me spend my money,
Make me feel real loose
Like a long-necked goose,
Like a girl.

Spoken:
Oh, baby,
That's-a what I like.

Charlie Brown

Words and Music by Jerry Leiber and Mike Stoller

recorded by The Coasters

Fee fee fi fi fo fo fum,
I smell smoke in the auditorium.

Refrain:
Charlie Brown, Charlie Brown,
He's a clown, that Charlie Brown.
He's gonna get caught, just you wait and see.
"Why is ev'rybody always pickin' on me?"

That's him on his knees, I know that's him,
Yellin' "Seven come eleven" down in the boys' gym.

Refrain
Who's always writin' on the walls?
Who's always goofin' in the halls?
Who's always throwin' spitballs?
Guess who? "Who, me?" Yeah, you!

Who walks in the classroom cool and slow?
Who calls the English teacher daddy-o?

Refrain

Come Go with Me

Words and Music by C.E. Quick

recorded by The Dell-Vikings

Love, love me, darling; come and go with me,
Please don't send me 'way beyond the sea;
I need you darlin'; so come go with me.

Come, come, come, come, come into my heart,
Tell me, darlin', we will never part;
I need you, darlin', so come go with me.

Yes, I need you, yes, I really need you,
Please say you'll never leave me.
Well say, you never yes, you really never;
You never give me a chance.

Come, come, come, come, come into my heart,
Tell me, darlin', we will never part;
I need you, darlin', so come go with me.

Cold, Cold Heart

Words and Music by Hank Williams

recorded by Hank Williams

I tried so hard, my dear, to show
That you're my ev'ry dream.
Yet you're afraid each thing I do
Is just some evil scheme.
A mem'ry from your lonesome past
Keeps us so far apart.
Why can't I free your doubtful mind
And melt your cold, cold heart?

Another love before my time
Made your heart sad and blue,
And so my heart is paying now
For things I didn't do.
In anger, unkind words are said
That make the teardrops start.
Why can't I free your doubtful mind
And melt your cold, cold heart?

You'll never know how much it hurts
To see you sit and cry.
You know you need and want my love,
Yet you're afraid to try.
Why do you run and hide from life?
To try it just ain't smart.
Why can't I free your doubtful mind
And melt your cold, cold heart?

There was a time when I believed
That you belonged to me.
But now I know your heart is shackled
To a memory.
The more I learn to care for you,
The more we drift apart.
Why can't I free your doubtful mind
And melt your cold, cold heart?

Cry

Words and Music by Churchill Kohlman

recorded by Johnnie Ray

If your sweetheart sends a letter of goodbye,
It's no secret you'll feel better if you cry.
When waking from a bad dream
Don't you sometimes think it's real?
But it's only false emotions that you feel!

If your heartaches seem to hang around too long,
And your blues keep getting bluer with each song
Remember, sunshine can be found behind a cloudy sky,
So let your hair down and go on and cry.

Cry Me a River

Words and Music by Arthur Hamilton

recorded by Julie London

Now you say you're lonely,
You cry the long night through,
Well, you can cry me a river,
Cry me a river.
I cried over you.

Now you say you're sorry
For bein' so untrue,
Well, you can cry me a river,
Cry me a river.
I cried a river over you.

You drove me,
Nearly drove me out of my head,
While you never shed a tear.
Remember?
I remember all that you said;
Told me love was too plebeian,
Told me you were through with me, an'

Now you say you love me,
Well, just to prove you do,
Come on an' cry me a river,
Cry me a river.
I cried a river over you.

The Deck of Cards

Words and Music by T. Texas Tyler

recorded by Wink Martindale

Spoken:
During the North-African campaign
A bunch of soldier boys had been on a long hike.
They arrived in a little town called Cassino
And the next day being Sunday, several of the boys went to church.
After the Chaplain read the prayer the text was taken up.
Those of the boys who had prayer books took them out
But one boy had only a deck of cards, so he spread them out.

The sergeant who commanded the boys saw the cards and said,
"Soldier, put away those cards."
After service was over the soldier was taken prisoner
And brought before the provost marshal.
The Marshal said, "Sergeant, why have you brought this man here?"
"For playing cards in church, Sir."
And what have you to say for yourself, son?"
"Much, Sir," the soldier replied.
The Marshal said, "I hope so, for if not I shall punish you severely."
The soldier said, "You see, sir, I have been on the march for six days
And I had neither bible not prayer book,
But I hope to satisfy you, Sir, with the purity of my intentions.

You see, Sir, when I look at the Ace it reminds me there is but one God.
And when I see the Deuce it reminds me that the Bible is divided
Into two parts, the Old and the New Testaments.
And when I see the Trey I think of the Father,
    the Son and the Holy Ghost.

And when I see the Four, I think of the four evangelists
Who preached the gospel, there were Matthew, Mark, Luke and John.
And when I see the Five it reminds me of the five Wise Virgins
Who trimmed their lamps. There were ten of them,
Five were wise and were saved, and five were foolish and shut out,
And when I see the Six it reminds me that in six days
God made this great Heaven and Earth,
And when I see the Seven it reminds me that on the seventh day God
    rested,
And when I see the Eight I think of the eight righteous persons
God saved when he destroyed this earth.
There were Noah, his wife, their three sons and their wives.

And when I see the Nine I think of the lepers our Savior cleansed
And the nine of the ten didn't even thank him.
When I see Ten I think of the Ten Commandments God handed to
    Moses
On the tablet of stone, and when I see the King it reminds me once
    again
There is but one king of Heaven, God Almighty,
And when I see the Queen, I think of the blessed Virgin Mary,
Who is Queen of Heav'n, and the Jack or Knave is the Devil.

And when I count the number on a deck of cards
I find three hundred and sixty-five, the number of days in a year.*
There are fifty two cards, the number of weeks in a year.
There are thirteen tricks, the number of weeks in a quarter.
There are four suits, the number of weeks in a month.
There are twelve picture cards, the number of months in a year.
So you see, Sir, my deck of cards has served me
As a Bible, Almanac and prayer book.
And, friends, this story is true. I know, because I was that soldier.

*Count the spots 1 to 10, the Jack as 11, the Queen as 12, King as 13 and Joker as 1.

Diana

Words and Music by Paul Anka

recorded by Paul Anka

I'm so young and you're so old.
This my darling I've been told.
I don't care just what they say
'Cause forever I will pray
You and I will be as free
As the birds up in the trees.
Oh please stay by me, Diana.

Thrills I get when you hold me close.
Oh my darling you're the most.
I love you but do you love me?
Oh Diana, can't you see
I love you with all my heart
And I hope we will never part.
Oh please stay with me, Diana.

Oh my darlin', oh my lover,
Tell me that there is no other.
I love you with my heart.
Oh oh, oh oh, oh oh.

Only you can take my heart.
Only you can tear it apart.
When you hold me in your loving arms
I can feel you giving all your charms.
Hold me darling, hold me tight.
Squeeze me baby with all your might.
Oh please stay by me, Diana. Oh please, Diana.

The Diary

Words and Music by Howard Greenfield and Neil Sedaka

recorded by Neil Sedaka

How I'd like to look into that little book,
The one that has the lock and key,
And know the boy that you care for,
The boy who's in your diary.

When it's late at night, what is the name you write?
Oh, what I'd give if I could see.
Am I the boy that you care for,
The boy who's in your diary?

Do you recall and make note of all
The little things I say and do?
The name you underline, I'm hoping that it's mine.
Darling, I'm so in love with you.

Please don't leave me blue. Make all my dreams come true.
You know how much you mean to me.
Say I'm the boy that you care for,
The boy who's in your diary.

Do You Want to Dance?

Words and Music by Bobby Freeman

recorded by Bobby Freeman

Do you want to dance and hold my hand?
Tell me you're my lover man.
Oh, baby, do you want to dance?

We could dance under the moonlight;
Hug and kiss all through the night.
Oh, baby, tell me, do you want to dance with me, baby?
Do you, do you, do you, do you want to dance?

Do you, do you, do you want to dance?
Do you, do you, do you, do you want to dance with me baby?
Ah, that's right! Ah, ah, ah.

Do you dance? Well, do you want to dance and to make romance?
Kiss and squeeze? Mm yes!
Do you want to dance?

Do you, do you, do you, do you wanna dance?
Do you, do you, do you, do you wanna dance?
Do you, do you, do you, do you want to dance?

Don't

Words and Music by Jerry Leiber and Mike Stoller

recorded by Elvis Presley

Don't, don't, that's what you say
Each time that I hold you this way.
When I feel like this and I want to kiss you,
Baby, don't say don't.

Don't, don't leave my embrace,
For here in my arms is your place.
When the night grows cold and I want to hold you,
Baby, don't say don't.

If you think that this is just a game I'm playing,
If you think that I don't mean ev'ry word I'm saying,
Don't, don't, don't feel that way.
I'm your love and yours I will stay.

This you can believe;
I will never leave you,
Heaven knows I won't.
Baby, don't say don't.

Don't Be Cruel
(To a Heart That's True)

Words and Music by Otis Blackwell and Elvis Presley

recorded by Elvis Presley

Refrain:
Don't be cruel to a heart that's true.
Don't be cruel to a heart that's true.
I don't want no other love.
Baby, it's just you I'm thinking of.

You known I can be found
Sitting all alone.
If you can't come around,
At least please telephone.
Don't be cruel to a heart that's true.

Baby, if I made you mad
For something I might have said,
Please, let's forget the past
'Cause the future looks bright ahead.
Don't be cruel to a heart that's true.

I don't want no other love,
Baby, it's just you I'm thinking of.

Well don't stop thinkin' of me.
Don't make me feel this way.
Come on over here and love me.
You know I wanna say
Don't be cruel to a heart that's true.

Why should we be apart?
I really, really love you,
Baby, cross my heart.

Let's walk up to the preacher
And let us say, "I do."
And then you'll know you have me,
And I'll know I have you too.
Don't be cruel to a heart that's true.

I don't want no other love.
Baby, it's just you I'm thinking of.

Refrain

Don't Let the Stars Get in Your Eyes

Words and Music by Slim Willet

recorded by Skeets McDonald, Ray Price

Don't let the stars get in your eyes,
Don't let the moon break your heart.
Love blooms at night, in daylight it dies;
Don't let the stars get in your eyes.
Oh keep your heart for me,
For someday I'll return and you know
You're the only one I'll ever love.

Too many nights, too many stars,
Too many moons could change your mind.
If I'm gone too long, don't forget where you belong;
When the stars come out, remember you are mine.

Don't let the stars get in your eyes,
Don't let the moon break your heart.
Love blooms at night, in daylight it dies;
Don't let the stars get in your eyes.
Oh keep your heart for me,
For someday I'll return and you know
You're the only one I'll ever love.

Donna

Words and Music by Ritchie Valens

recorded by Ritchie Valens

Oh, Donna, oh, Donna,
Oh, Donna, oh, Donna.

I had a girl, Donna was her name,
Since she left me I've never been the same,
'Cause I love my girl, Donna where can you be,
Where can you be?

Now that you're gone, I'm left all alone,
All by myself to wander and roam,
'Cause I love my girl, Donna where can you be,
Where can you be?

Oh, darlin' now that you're gone
I don't know what I'll do.
All my smiles and all my love for you.

I had a girl, Donna was her name,
Since she left me I've never been the same,
'Cause I love my girl, Donna where can you be,
Where can you be?

Repeat and fade:
Oh, Donna, oh, Donna,
Oh, Donna, oh, Donna.

Dream Lover

Words and Music by Bobby Darin

recorded by Bobby Darin

Ev'ry night I hope and pray
A dream lover will come my way,
A girl to hold in my arms
And know the magic of her charms.
Because I want a girl to call my own,
I want a dream lover so I don't have to dream alone.

Dream lover, where are you,
With a love, oh, so true
And a hand that I can hold
To feel you near when I grow old?
Because I want a girl to call my own,
I want a dream lover so I don't have to dream alone.

Someday, I don't know how,
I hope you'll hear my plea.
Some way, I don't know how,
She'll bring her love to me.

Dream lover, until then,
I'll go to sleep and dream again.
That's the only thing to do
Until my lover's dreams come true.
Because I want a girl to call my own,
I want a dream lover so I don't have to dream alone.

Earth Angel

Words and Music by Jesse Belvin

recorded by The Crew-Cuts

Earth angel, earth angel,
Will you be mine,
My darling, dear, love you all the time.
I'm just a fool, a fool in love with you.

Earth angel, earth angel,
The one I adore, love you forever and evermore.
I'm just a fool, a fool in love with you.

I fell for you,
And I knew the vision of your love's loveliness,
I hope and I pray
That someday I'll be the vision of your happiness.

Earth angel, earth angel,
Please be mine, my darling dear, love you all the time.
I'm just a fool, a fool in love with you.

Endlessly

Words and Music by Clyde Otis and Brook Benton

recorded by Brook Benton

Higher than the highest mountain
And deeper than the deepest sea,
That's how I will love you, darling, endlessly.

Softer than the gentle breezes
And stronger than a wild oak tree,
That's how I will hold you, darling, endlessly.

Oh, my love, you are my heaven,
You are my kingdom, you are my crown.
Oh, my love, you're all I prayed for;
You were made for these arms to surround.

Faithful as a morning sunrise
And sacred as a love can be,
That's how I will love you, darling, endlessly.

Repeat and fade:
Endlessly

Everyday

Words and Music by Norman Petty and Charles Hardin

recorded by Buddy Holly

Ev'ry day it's a-getting closer,
Going faster than a roller coaster.
Love like yours will truly come my way.

Ev'ry day it's a-getting faster,
Ev'ryone said, "Go on up and ask her."
Love like yours will truly come my way.

Ev'ry day seems a little longer.
Ev'ry way love's a little stronger.
Come what may,
Do you ever long for true love from me?

Ev'ry day it's a-getting closer,
Going faster than a roller coaster.
Love like yours will truly come my way.

Fever

Words and Music by John Davenport and Eddie Cooley

recorded by Peggy Lee

Never know how much I love you,
Never know how much I care.
When you put your arms around me,
I get fever that's so hard to bear.

Refrain:
You give me fever
When you kiss me,
Fever when you hold me tight.
Fever in the morning,
Fever all through the night.

Sun lights up the daytime,
Moon lights up the night.
I light up when you call my name,
And you know I'm gonna treat you right.

Refrain

Everybody's got the fever
That is something you all know.
Fever isn't such a new thing,
Fever started long ago.

Romeo loved Juliet,
Juliet, she felt the same,
When he put his arms around her, he said,
"Julie, baby, you're my flame."

Thou givest fever, when we kisseth
Fever with thy flaming youth,
Fever—I'm afire
Fever, Yea, I burn forsooth.

Captain Smith and Pocahontas
Had a very mad affair,
When her Daddy tried to kill him, she said,
"Daddy-o, don't you dare."

Give me fever, with his kisses,
Fever when he holds me tight.
Fever—I'm his Missus
Oh Daddy won't you treat him right.

Now you've listened to my story
Here's the point that I have made:
Chicks were born to give you fever
Be it Fahrenheit or centigrade.

They give you fever when you kiss them,
Fever if you live and learn.
Fever—till you sizzle
What a lovely way to burn.

(Now and Then There's) A Fool Such as I

Words and Music by Bill Trader

recorded by Elvis Presley, Hank Snow

Pardon me, if I'm sentimental when we say goodbye.
Don't be angry with me should I cry.
When you're gone, yet I'll dream a little dream
As years go by.
Now and then, there's a fool such as I.
Now and then, there's a fool such as I am over you.
You taught me how to love,
And now you say that we are through.
I'm a fool, but I'll love you, dear,
Until the day I die.
Now and then, there's a fool such as I.

Friendly Persuasion

Words by Paul Francis Webster
Music by Dimitri Tiomkin

recorded by Pat Boone

Thee I love.
More that the meadow so green and still,
More than the mulberries on the hill,
More than the buds on the May apples tree,
I love thee.
Arms have I, strong as the oak, for this occasion.
Lips have I to kiss thee, too, in friendly persuasion.
Thee is mine, though I don't know many words of praise.
Thee pleasures me In a hundred ways.
Put on your bonnet, your cape, and your glove,
And come with me, for thee I love.

Goodnight My Love, Pleasant Dreams

Words and Music by George Motola and John Marascalco

recorded by The McGuire Sisters

Goodnight, my love,
Pleasant dreams and sleep tight, my love.
May tomorrow be sunny and bright
And bring you closer to me.

Before you go
Please remember I need you so,
And this love I have for you
Will never grow cold.

If you should awake in the still of the night,
Please have no fear.
Just close your eyes, then you'll realize
That my love will watch over you, dear, always.

Repeat Verse 1

Great Balls of Fire

Words and Music by Otis Blackwell and Jack Hammer

recorded by Jerry Lee Lewis

You shake my nerves and you rattle my brain.
Too much love drives a man insane.
You broke my will,
But what a thrill.
Goodness gracious, great balls of fire!

I laughed at love 'cause I thought it was funny.
You came along and you moved me, honey.
I changed my mind,
Love's just fine.
Goodness gracious, great balls of fire!

Kiss me, baby.
Woo, it feels good.
Hold me, baby.
Girl just let me love you like a lover should.
You're fine, so kind,
I'm gonna tell the world that you're mine, mine, mine.

I chew my nails and I twiddle my thumb.
I'm nervous but it sure is fun.
Come on, baby, you're driving me crazy.
Goodness gracious, great balls of fire.

The Great Pretender

Words and Music by Buck Ram

recorded by The Platters

Oh yes, I'm the great pretender,
Pretendin' I'm doin' well;
My need is such, I pretend too much,
I'm lonely but no one can tell.

Oh yes, I'm the great pretender,
Adrift in a world of my own;
I play the game but, to my real shame,
You've left me to dream alone,

Too real is this feeling of make believe,
Too real when I feel what my heart can't conceal;

Oh, yes, I'm the great pretender,
Just laughin' and gay like a clown;
I seem to be what I'm not, you see,
I'm wearin' my heart like a crown;
Pretendin' that you're still aroun'.

The Green Door

Words and Music by Bob Davie and Marvin Moore

recorded by Jim Lowe

Midnight, one more night without sleepin',
Watching till the morning comes peepin',
Green door, what's the secret you're keepin'?
There's an old piano, and they play it hot
Behind the green door.
Don't know what they're doin', but they laugh a lot
Behind the green door.
Wish they'd let me in so I could find out what's
Behind the green door.

Knocked once, tried to tell 'em I'd been there.
Door slammed, hospitality's thin there.
Wonder just what's goin' on in there.
Saw an eyeball peepin' through a smoky cloud
Behind the green door.
When I said Joe sent me, someone laughed out loud
Behind the green door.
All I want to do is join the happy crew
Behind the green door.

Happy, Happy Birthday Baby

Words and Music by Margo Sylvia and Gilbert Lopez

recorded by The Tune Weavers

Happy, happy birthday baby.
Although you're with somebody new,
Thought I'd drop a line to say
That I wish this happy day
Would find me beside you.

Happy, happy birthday baby.
No, I can't call you my baby.
Seems like years ago we met
On a day I can't forget,
'Cause that's when we fell in love.

Do you remember the names we had for each other?
You were my pretty, I was your baby.
How could we say good-bye?

Hope I didn't spoil your birthday.
I know I'm acting kind of crazy,
So I'll close this note to you
With good luck and wishes too.
Happy, happy birthday baby.

Do you remember the names we had for each other?
You were my pretty, I was your baby.
How could we say good-bye?

Hope I didn't spoil your birthday.
I know I'm acting kind of crazy,
So I'll close this note to you
With good luck and wishes too.
Happy, happy birthday baby.

Have I Told You Lately That I Love You

Words and Music by Scott Wiseman

recorded by Ricky Nelson

Have I told you lately that I love you?
Could I tell you once again somehow?
Have I told with all my heart and soul how I adore you?
Well, darling, I'm telling you now.
(I'm telling you, telling you.)

Have I told you lately when I'm sleeping
Ev'ry dream I dream is you somehow?
Have I told you why the nights are long when you're not with me?
Well, darling, I'm telling you now.
(I'm telling you.)

My heart would break in two if I should lose you.
I'm no good without you anyhow.
Dear, have I told you lately that I love you?
Well, darling, I'm telling you now.
(I'm telling you, telling you now.)

Well, darling, I'm telling you now.
(I'm telling you, telling you now.)

He

Words by Richard Mullen
Music by Jack Richards

recorded by Al Hibbler, The McGuire Sisters

He can turn the tides and calm the angry sea;
He alone decides who writes a symphony;
He lights ev'ry star that makes our darkness bright,
He keeps watch all through each long and lonely night.

He still finds the time to hear a child's first prayer;
Saint or sinner call and always find him there.
Though it makes him sad to see the way we live,
He'll always say, "I forgive."

He can grant a wish or make a dream come true,
He can paint the clouds and turn the gray to blue;
He alone knows where to find the rainbow's end,
He alone can see what lies beyond the bend.

He can touch a tree and turn the leaves to gold,
He knows ev'ry lie that you and I have told.
Though it makes him sad to see the way we live,
He'll always say, "I forgive, I forgive."

The Hawaiian Wedding Song (Ke Kali Nei Au)

English Lyrics by Al Hoffman and Dick Manning
Hawaiian Lyrics and Music by Charles E. King

recorded by Andy Williams

This is the moment I've waited for.
I can hear my heart singing,
Soon bells will be ringing.
This is the moment of sweet aloha,
I will love you longer than forever,
Promise that you will leave me never.
Here and now, dear,
All my love I vow, dear,
Promise me that you will leave me never,
I will love you longer than forever.
Now that we are one, clouds won't hide the sun.
Blue skies of Hawaii smile on this, our wedding day.
I do love you with all my heart.

Hawaiian Lyric:
Eia au ke kali nei
Aia la i hea kuu aloha
Eia au ke huli nei
A loaa oe e ka ipo
Maha ka iini a ka puuwai
Ua sila' paa ia me oe
Ko aloha makamae e ipo
Ka 'u ia e lei ae neila
Nou no ka iini
A nou wale no
A o ko aloha ka'u e hiipoi mau
Na'u oe nau'u oe, e lei e lei
Na'u oe e lei

A he halia kai hiki mai
No kuu lei onaona
Pulupe i ka ua
Auhea oe kaiini a loko
Nu loko ae ka manao
Hu'e luni ana i kuu kino
Kuu pua kuu lei onaona
A'u i kui a lawai a nei
Me ke ala pua pikake
A o oe kuu pua
Ku'u pua lei lehua
A'u e li'a mau nei hoopaa
Ia iho kealoha
He lei, he lei, oe na'u, oe na'u
He lei 'oe na'u

Heartbreak Hotel

Words and Music by Mae Boren Axton, Tommy Durden and Elvis Presley

recorded by Elvis Presley

Well, since my baby left me,
Well I found a new place to dwell,
Down at the end of Lonely Street,
At Heartbreak Hotel.
I'm so lonely,
I'm so lonely,
I'm so lonely that I could die.

And though it's overcrowded
You can still find some room
For broken-hearted lovers
To cry there in their gloom,
And be so lonely,
Oh, so lonely,
Oh, so lonely they could die.

The bellhop's tears are flowing,
The clerk's dressed in black.
They've been so long on Lonely Street
They never will go back.
And they're so lonely,
Oh, they're so lonely,
They're so lonely they pray to die.

So if your baby leaves you
And you have a tale to tell,
Just take a walk down Lonely Street
To Heartbreak Hotel
Where you'll be so lonely,
And I'll be so lonely,
We'll be so lonely that we could die.

Honeycomb

Words and Music by Bob Merrill

recorded by Jimmie Rodgers

Honeycomb, honeycomb.

Refrain:
Honeycomb, won't ya be my baby?
Honeycomb, be my own.
Just a hank of hair and a piece of bone
Made a walkin', talkin' honeycomb.
Honeycomb, won't ya be my baby?
Honeycomb, be my own.
What a darn good life
When I've got a wife like honeycomb.

It's a darn good life and it's kinda funny
How the bee was made and the bee made the honey,
The honeybee, lookin' for a home,
Made my honeycomb.

Then they roamed the world and they gathered all
Of the honeycomb into one sweet ball.
The honeycomb from a million trips
Made my baby's lips.

Refrain

Now have you heard tell how they made a bee,
Then tried a hand at a green, green tree?
So the tree was made and I guess you've heard,
Next they made a bird.
Then they went around lookin' everywhere,
Takin' love from here and from there,
And they stored it up in a little cart,
For my honey's heart.

Refrain

Heartaches by the Number

Words and Music by Harlan Howard

recorded by Guy Mitchell, Ray Price

Heartache number one was when you left me,
I never knew that I could hurt this way.
And heartache number two was when you came back again,
You came back and never meant to stay.

Refrain:
Now I've got heartaches by the number, troubles by the score.
Ev'ry day you love me less, each day I love you more.
Yes, I've got heartaches by the number, a love that I can't win,
But the day that I stop counting, that's the day my world will end.

Heartache number three was when you called me
And said that you were coming back to stay.
With hopeful heart I waited for your knock on the door,
I waited, but you must have lost your way.

Refrain

Hound Dog

Words and Music by Jerry Leiber and Mike Stoller

recorded by Elvis Presley

You ain't nothin' but a hound dog,
Cryin' all the time.
You ain't nothin' but a hound dog,
Cryin' all the time.
Well, you ain't never caught a rabbit
And you ain't no friend of mine.

When they said you was high-classed,
Well, that was just a lie.
When they said you was high-classed,
Well, that was just a lie.
Well, you ain't never caught a rabbit
And you ain't no friend of mine.

Hushabye

Words and Music by Doc Pomus and Mort Shuman

recorded by The Mystics

Hushabye, hushabye,
Oh my darlin', don't you cry.
Guardian angels up above
Take care of the one I love.
Ooh, ooh.
Ooh, ooh.

Pillows lying on your bed;
Oh, my darling, rest your head.
Sandman will be coming soon,
Singing you a slumber tune.
Ooh, ooh.
Ooh.

Lullaby and goodnight,
In your dreams I'll hold you tight.
Lullaby and goodnight,
Till the dawn's early light.

Repeat Verse 1

I Almost Lost My Mind

Words and Music by Ivory Joe Hunter

recorded by Pat Boone

When I lost my baby,
I almost lost my mind.
When I lost my baby,
I almost lost my mind.
My head is in a spin
Since she left me behind.

I pass a million people,
I can't tell who I meet.
I pass a million people,
I can't tell who I meet,
'Cause my eyes are full of tears.
Where can my baby be?

I went to see a gypsy
And had my fortune read.
I went to see a gypsy
And had my fortune read.
I hung my head in sorrow
When she said what she said.

I can tell you, people,
The news was not so good.
Well, I can tell you, people,
The news was not so good.
She said, "Your baby has quit you.
This time she's gone for good."

I Beg of You

Words and Music by Rose Marie McCoy and Kelly Owens

recorded by Elvis Presley

I don't want my heart to be broken
'Cause it's the only one I've got.
So, darling, please be careful;
You know I care a lot.
Darling, please don't break my heart,
I beg of you.

I don't want no tears a-falling;
You know I hate to cry,
But that's what's bound to happen
If you ever say goodbye.
Darling please don't say goodbye,
I beg of you.

Hold my hand and promise that
You'll always love me true.
Make me know you love me
The same way I love you, little girl.

You got me at your mercy
Now that I'm in love with you.
So, please don't take advantage
'Cause you know my love is true.
My darling, please, please love me, too,
I beg of you.

I Believe

Words and Music by Ervin Drake, Irvin Graham, Jimmy Shirl and Al Stillman

a standard recorded by various artists

I believe for every drop of rain that falls,
A flower grows.
I believe that somewhere in the darkest night,
A candle glows.
I believe for everyone who goes astray,
Someone will come
To show the way.
I believe.

I believe above the storm the smallest prayer
Will still be heard.
I believe that someone in the great somewhere
Hears every word.
Every time I hear a new-born baby cry
Or touch a leaf,
Or see the sky
I believe
Then I know why
I believe!

I Can't Help It
(If I'm Still in Love with You)

Words and Music by Hank Williams

recorded by Hank Williams

Refrain:
Today I passed you on the street,
And my heart fell at your feet.
I can't help it if I'm still in love with you.
Somebody else stood by your side,
And he looked so satisfied.
I can't help it if I'm still in love with you.

A picture from the past came slowly stealing
As I brushed your arm and walked so close to you.
Then suddenly I got that old-time feeling.
I can't help it if I'm still in love with you.

Refrain

It's hard to know another's lips will kiss you
And hold you just the way I used to do.
Oh, heaven only knows how much I miss you.
I can't help it if I'm still in love with you.

('Til) I Kissed You

Words and Music by Don Everly

recorded by The Everly Brothers

Never felt like this until I kissed you.
How did I exist until I kissed you?
Never had you on my mind;
Now you're there all the time.
Never knew what I missed until I kissed you.
Uh-huh, I kissed you, oh yeah.

Things have really changed since I kissed you.
My life's not the same now that I kissed you.
Mmm, you got a way about you;
Now I can't live without you.
Never knew what I missed until I kissed you.
Uh-huh, I kissed you, oh yeah.

You don't realize what you do to me.
And I didn't realize what a kiss could be.
Mmm, you got a way about you;
Now I can't live without you.
Never knew what I missed until I kissed you.
Uh-huh, I kissed you,
Oh yeah, I kissed you.

I Said My Pajamas
(And Put on My Pray'rs)

Words and Music by Eddie Pola and George Wyle

recorded by Tony Martin & Fran Warren

My baby kissed me goodnight,
And I am glad to relate
That by the time I got home,
I was feeling great!

I climbed up the door and opened the stairs.
I said my pajamas and put on my prayers.
I turned off the bed and crawled into the light,
And all because you kissed me goodnight.

Next morning I woke and scrambled my shoes.
I shined up an egg, then I toasted the news.
I buttered my tie and took another bite,
And all because you kissed me goodnight.

By evening I felt normal,
So we went out again.
You said, "Goodnight," and kissed me,
I hurried home, and then

I climbed up the door and opened the stairs.
I said my pajamas and put on my prayers
I turned off the bed and crawled into the light,
And all because you kissed me goodnight.

I powdered my hair and pinned up my nose.
I hung up the bath and I turned on my clothes.
I put out the clock and wound the cat up tight,
And all because you kissed me goodnight.

I ran up the shade and pulled down the stair.
I curled up the rug and I vacuumed my hair.
I just couldn't tell my left foot from my right,
And all because you kissed me goodnight.

By evening I felt normal,
So we went out again.
You said, "Goodnight," and kissed me.
I hurried home, and then

I lifted the preacher and called up the phone.
I spoke to the dog and I threw your ma a bone.
'Twas midnight and yet
The sun was shining bright,
And all because you kissed me goodnight.

I Walk the Line

Words and Music by John R. Cash

recorded by Johnny Cash

I keep a close watch on this heart of mine.
I keep my eyes wide open all the time.
I keep the ends out for the ties that bind.
Because you're mine,
I walk the line.

I find it very, very easy to be true.
I find myself alone when each day is through.
Yes, I'll admit that I'm a fool for you.
Because you're mine,
I walk the line.

As sure as night is dark and day is light,
I keep you on my mind both day and night.
And happiness I've known proves that it's right.
Because you're mine,
I walk the line.

You've got a way to keep me on your side.
You give me a cause for love that I can't hide.
For you, I know, I'd even try to turn the tide.
Because you're mine,
I walk the line.

I keep a close watch on this heart of mine.
I keep my eyes wide open all of the time.
I keep the ends out for the ties that bind.
Because you're mine,
I walk the line.

I Want You, I Need You, I Love You

Words by Maurice Mysels
Music by Ira Kosloff

recorded by Elvis Presley

Hold me close, hold me tight;
Make me thrill with delight.
Let me know where I stand from the start.
I want you, I need you, I love you with all my heart.

Ev'ry time that you're near
All my cares disappear.
Darling, you're all that I'm livin' for.
I want you, I need you, I love you more and more.

I thought I could live without romance
Before you came to me,
But now I know that I will go
On loving you eternally.

Won't you please be my own?
Never leave me alone,
'Cause I die ev'ry time we're apart.
I want you, I need you, I love you with all my heart.

I'll Be Home

Words and Music by Ferdinand Washington and Stan Lewis

recorded by Pat Boone

I'll be home, my darling,
Please wait for me.
We'll stroll along together.
Once more our love will be free.

At the corner drug store,
Each Saturday we would meet;
I'd walk you home in the moonlight,
All of these things we'll repeat.

So darling, as I write this letter,
Here's hoping you're thinking of me;
My mind's made up,
So long, until I'll be home to start serving you.

I'll be home, my darling,
Please wait for me.
I'll walk you home in the moonlight,
Once more our love will be free.

I'll Drown in My Tears

Words and Music by Henry Glover

recorded by Ray Charles

It brings a tear into my eyes
When I begin to realize.
I've cried so much since you've been gone.
I guess I'll drown in my own tears.

I sit and cry just like a child.
My pourin' tears are runnin' wild.
If you don't think you'll be home soon,
I guess I'll drown, oh, yes, in my own tears.

I know it's true, into each life
Some rain, rain must pour,
I'm so blue here without you.
It keeps a-rainin' more and more.

Why can't you come on home,
Oh, yeah, so I won't be all alone?
If you don't think you'll be home soon,
I guess I'll drown in my own tears.

Don't let me drown in my own tears.
When I'm in trouble, (drown in my own tears)
Don't let me drown in my own tears.
I guess I'll drown in my own tears.
Oh, ooh.

I'm Stickin' with You

Words and Music by Dave Alldred, James Bowen, Buddy Knox and Donnie Lanier

recorded by Jimmy Bowen

Refrain:
Be bop, I love you, baby.
Be bop, I don't mean maybe.
Be bop, I love you, baby.
I'm stickin' with you.
I'm stickin' with you.

Years may come and a-go.
I will love you so.
No matter where we go,
I'm stickin' with you.
I'm stickin' with you.

New loves may come your way,
But my love's here to stay.
This is why I say,

Refrain

New loves may come your way, But my love's here to stay.
    This is why I say,

Refrain

I'm Walking Behind You
(Look Over Your Shoulder)

Words and Music by Billy Reid

recorded by Eddie Fisher

I'm walking behind you on your wedding day
And I'll hear you promise to love and obey.
Though you may forget me, you're still on my mind;
Look over your shoulder; I'm walking behind.

Maybe I'll kiss again with a love that's new,
But I shall wish again I was kissing you.

'Cause I'll always love you wherever you go,
And though we are parted I want you to know
That if things go wrong, dear, and fate is unkind,
Look over your shoulder, I'm walking behind.

If

Words by Robert Hargreaves and Stanley J. Damerell
Music by Tolchard Evans

a standard recorded by various artists

If they made me a king, I'd be a slave to you.
If I had ev'rything, I'd still be a slave to you.
If I ruled the night, stars and moon so right,
Still I'd turn for light to you.

If the world to me bowed, yet humbly I'll plead to you.
If my friends were a crowd, I'd turn in my need to you.
If I ruled the earth, what would life be worth
If I hadn't the right to you?

It's Almost Tomorrow

Words and Music by Wade Buff and Gene Adkinson

recorded by The Dream Weavers

My dearest, my darling, tomorrow is near.
The sun will bring showers of sadness, I fear.
Your lips won't be smiling, your eyes will not shine,
For I know tomorrow that your love won't be mine.

It's almost tomorrow, but what can I do?
Your kisses all tell me that your love is untrue.
I'll love you forever till stars cease to shine,
And hope someday, darling, that you'll always be mine.

Your heart was so warm, dear, it now has turned cold.
You no longer love me, for your mem'ries grow old.
It's almost tomorrow, for here comes the sun,
But still I am hoping that tomorrow won't come.

It's almost tomorrow, but what can I do?
Your kisses all tell me that your love is untrue.
I'll love you forever till stars cease to shine,
And hope someday, darling, that you'll always be mine.

If You Love Me, Really Love Me (Hymne a l'amour)

English Words by Geoffrey Parsons
French Words by Edith Piaf
Music by Marguerite Monnot

recorded by Kaye Starr

If the sun should tumble from the sky,
If the sea should suddenly run dry,
If you love me, really love me,
Let it happen, I won't care.

If it seems that ev'rything is lost,
I will smile and never count the cost.
If you love me, really love me,
Let it happen, darling, I won't care.

Shall I catch a shooting star?
Shall I bring it where you are?
If you want me to, I will.
You can set me any task.
I'll do anything you ask,
If you'll only love me still.

When at last our life on earth is through,
I will share eternity with you.
If you love me, really love me,
Then whatever happens, I won't care.

French lyrics:
Le ciel bleu sur nous peut s'ecrouler,
Et la terre peut bien s'effondrer
Peu m'importe si tu m'aimes,
Je me moque du monde entier.

Tant qu'l'amour inondra mes matins,
Que mon corps fremira sous tes mains,
Peu m'inporte les grands problemes,
Mon amour puisque tu m'aimes.

J'irais jus qu'au bout du monde,
Je me ferais teindre blonde,
Si tu me le demandais.
On peut bien rire de moi,
Je ferais n'im porte quoi,
Si tu me le demandais.

Nous aurons pour nous l'eternite,
Dans le blue de toute l'immensite
Dans le ciel plus de problemes,
Dieu reunit ceux qui s'aiment.

In the Still of the Nite (I'll Remember)

Words and Music by Fred Parris

recorded by The Five Satins

(Shoo doop doo be doo,
Shoo doop shoo be doo,
Shoo doop shoo be doo.
Shoo doop shoo be wah.)

In the still of the nite
I held you, held you tight.
Oh, I love, love you so,
Promise I'll never let you go
In the still of the nite.
(In the still of the nite.)

I remember that nite in May
That the stars were bright up above.
I'll hope and I'll pray
To keep your precious love.

So, before the light,
Hold me again with all of your might
In the still of the nite.
(In the still of the nite.)

(Shoo wop shoo wah,
Shoo wop shoo wah,
Shoo wop shoo wah,
Shoo wop shoo wah.)

So before the light,
Hold me again
With all of your might
In the still of the nite.

(In the still of the nite.)

In the still of the nite.
(Shoo doop doo be doo,
Shoo doop shoo be doo,
Shoo doop shoo be doo.
Shoo doop shoo be wah.)…

It's Just a Matter of Time

Words and Music by Clyde Otis, Brook Benton and Belford Hendricks

recorded by Brook Benton

Someday, someday you'll realize that you've been blind.
Yes, darling, you're going to need me again;
It's just a matter of time.

Go on, go on until you reach the end of the line.
But I know you'll pass this way again;
It's just a matter of time.

After I gave you ev'rything I had,
You laughed and called me a clown.
Remember in your search for fortune and fame,
What goes up must come down.

I know, I know that one day you'll wake up and find
That my love was a true love;
It's just a matter of time.

It's Not for Me to Say

Words by Al Stillman
Music by Robert Allen

recorded by Johnny Mathis

It's not for me to say you love me,
It's not for me to say you'll always care.
Oh, but here for the moment I can hold you fast,
And press your lips to mine, and dream that love will last.

As far as I can see, this is heaven,
And speaking just for me, it's ours to share.
Perhaps the glow of love will grow with ev'ry passing day,
Or we may never meet again, but then it's not for me to say.

It's Only Make Believe

Words and Music by Conway Twitty and Jack Nance

recorded by Conway Twitty

People see us everywhere, they think you really care,
But myself I can't deceive, I know it's only make believe.
My one and only prayer, is that someday you'll care.

My hopes, my dreams come true, my one and only you,
No one will ever know, how much I love you so,
My only prayer will be, someday you'll care for me,
But it's only make believe.

My hopes, my dreams come true, my life I'd give for you,
My heart, a wedding ring, my all, my everything.
My heart I can't control, you rule my very soul,
My plans, my hopes, my schemes, you are my everything,
But it's only make believe.

My one and only prayer is that someday you'll care,
My hopes, my dreams come true, my one and only you.
No one will ever know, just how much I love you so,
My only prayer will be that someday you'll care for me
But it's only make believe.

It's So Easy

Words and Music by Buddy Holly and Norman Petty

recorded by The Crickets

Refrain:
It's so easy to fall in love.
It's so easy to fall in love.

People tell me love's for fools,
So here I go breaking all the rules.
It seems so easy, so dog-gone easy;
It seems so easy where you're concerned.
My heart has learned.

Refrain

Look into your heart and see
What your love book has set apart for me.
It seems so easy, so dog-gone easy;
It seems so easy where you're concerned.
My heart has learned.

Refrain

Ivory Tower

Words and Music by Jack Fulton and Lois Steele

recorded by Cathy Carr, Gale Storm

Come down, come down from your ivory tower,
Let love come into your heart.
Don't lock yourself in an ivory tower,
Don't keep us so far apart.
I love you, I love you.
Are you too far above me to hear?
Come down, come down from your ivory tower,
You'll find true love has its charms.
It's cold, so cold in your ivory tower,
And warm, so warm in my arms.

Jambalaya (On the Bayou)

Words and Music by Hank Williams

recorded by Hank Williams

Good-bye, Joe, me gotta go, me oh my oh.
Me gotta go pole the pirogue down the bayou.
My Yvonne, the sweetest one, me oh my oh,
Son of a gun, we'll have big fun on the bayou.

Refrain:
Jambalaya and a crawfish pie and fillet gumbo,
'Cause tonight I'm gonna see my ma cher amie-o.
Pick guitar, fill fruit jar, and be gay-o.
Son of a gun, we'll have big fun on the bayou.

Thibodaux, Fontaineaux, the place is buzzin'.
Kinfolk come to see Yvonne by the dozen.
Dress in style and go hog wild, me oh my oh.
Son of a gun, we'll have big fun on the bayou.

Refrain

Settle down far from town, get me a pirogue,
And I'll catch all the fish in the bayou.
Swap my mon to buy Yvonne what she need-o.
Son of a gun, we'll have big fun on the bayou.

Refrain

Jailhouse Rock

Words and Music by Jerry Leiber and Mike Stoller

recorded by Elvis Presley

The warden threw a party in the county jail.
The prison band was there and they began to wail.
The band was jumpin' and the joint began to swing.
You should've heard those knocked-out jailbirds sing.

Refrain:
Let's rock!
Everybody, let's rock!
Everybody in the whole cell block
Was a-dancin' to the Jailhouse Rock.
Spider Murphy played the tenor saxophone.
Little Joe was blowin' on the slide trombone.
The drummer boy from Illinois went crash, boom, bang:
The whole rhythm section was the Purple Gang.

Refrain

Number Forty-Seven said to Number Three,
"You're the cutest little jailbird I ever did see.
I sure would be delighted with your company.
Come on and do the Jailhouse Rock with me."

Refrain

The sad sack was a-sittin' on a block of stone,
Way over in the corner weeping all alone.
The warden said, "Hey buddy, don't you be no square.
If you can't find a partner use a wooden chair!"

Refrain

Shifty Henry said to Bugs, "For heaven's sake,
No one's lookin'; now's our chance to make a break."
Bugsy turned to Shifty and he said, "Nix, nix;
I wanna stick around awhile and get my kicks."

Refrain

Just a Dream

Words and Music by Big Bill Broonzy

recorded by Jimmy Clanton

It was a dream.
Lord, what a dream I had on my mind.
It was a dream.
Lord, what a dream I had on my mind.
Now and when I woke up, baby,
Not a thing there could I find.

I dreamed I went out with an angel and had a good time.
I dreamed I was satisfied and nothin' to worry my mind.
But that was just a dream.
Lord, what a dream I had on my mind.
Now and when I woke up, baby,
Not an angel could I find.

I dreamed I caught the horses and caught the numbers, too.
I dreamed I won so much money I didn't know what to do.
But that was just a dream.
Lord, what a dream I had on my mind.
Now and when I woke up, baby,
Not a penny there could I find.

I dreamed I was in the White House sittin' in the President's chair.
I dreamed he's shaking my hand and he said,
    "Bill, I'm so glad you're here."
But that was just a dream.
Lord, what a dream I had on my mind.
Now and when I woke up, baby,
Not a chair there could I find.

I dreamed I got married and started me a family.
I dreamed I had ten children and they all looked, just like me.
But that was just a dream.
Lord, what a dream I had on my mind.
Now and when I woke up, baby,
Not a child there looked like mine.

Just Walking in the Rain

Words and Music by Johnny Bragg and Robert S. Riley

recorded by Johnnie Ray

Just walking in the rain, getting soaking wet:
Torturing my heart by trying to forget.
Just walking in the rain, so alone and blue;
All because my heart still remembers you.

People come to windows and they always stare at me;
Shake their heads in sorrow, saying, "Who can that fool be?"
Just walking in the rain, thinking how we met;
Knowing things have changed, somehow I can't forget.

Kansas City

Words and Music by Jerry Leiber and Mike Stoller

recorded by Wilbert Harrison

I'm goin' to Kansas City, Kansas City here I come.
I'm goin' to Kansas City, Kansas City here I come.
They got a crazy way of lovin' there and I'm gonna get me some.

I'm gonna be standin' on the corner Twelfth Street and Vine.
I'm gonna be standin' on the corner Twelfth Street and Vine,
With my Kansas City baby and a bottle of Kansas City wine.
Well, I might take a train, I might take a plane,
But if I have to walk, I'm goin' just the same.

Refrain:
I'm goin' to Kansas City, Kansas City here I come.
They got a crazy way of lovin' there and I'm gonna get me some.

I'm goin' to pack my clothes, leave at the crack of dawn.
I'm goin' to pack my clothes, leave at the crack of dawn.
My old lady will be sleepin', she won't know where I'm gone.
'Cause if I stay with that woman, I know I'm gonna die.
Gotta find a brand-new baby, and that's the reason why.

Refrain

Keep It a Secret

Words and Music by Jessie Mae Robinson

a standard recorded by various artists

If you see my darling with somebody new,
Keep it a secret, whatever you do.
Why should you tell me and break my heart?
Then foolish pride would just drive us apart.

If you see my darling in some rendezvous,
Painting the town with a girl he once knew,
Pay no attention and just let it be,
But keep it a secret from me.

Lipstick on Your Collar

Words by Edna Lewis
Music by George Goehring

recorded by Connie Francis

When you left me all alone at the record hop,
Told me you were goin' out for a soda pop,
You were gone for quite a while,
Half an hour or more.
You came back and man, oh man,
This is what I saw.

Refrain:
Lipstick on your collar told a tale on you.
Lipstick on your collar said you were untrue.
Bet your bottom dollar you and I are through,
'Cause lipstick on your collar told a tale on you.

You said it belonged to me; made me stop and think.
Then I noticed yours was red, mine was baby pink.
Who walked in but Mary Jane, lipstick all a mess.
Were you smoochin' my best friend? Guess the answer's yes.

Refrain

Little Darlin'

Words and Music by Maurice Williams

recorded by The Diamonds

Little darlin', my little darlin', oh, where are you?
My love, I was wrong to try to love two,
Knowing well that my love was just for you, only you.

Spoken:
My dear, I need your love to call my own
And never do wrong; and to hold in mine your little hand.
I'll know too soon that I'll love again.
Please come back to me.

Little Star

Words and Music by Arthur Venosa and Vito Picone

recorded by The Elegants

Oh, ra ta ta ta ta.

Twinkle, twinkle, little star.
How I wonder where you are.
Wish I may, wish I might,
Make this wish come true tonight.
Searched all over for a love.
You're the one I'm thinking of.

Oh, ra ta ta ta tu.
Oh, ra ta ta ta tu.

Twinkle, twinkle, little star.
How I wonder where you are.
High above the clouds somewhere,
Send me down a love to share. Oh.

Oh there you are, high above.
Oh God, send me a love.
Oh there you are, hiding above the sky,
I need a love, oh me oh me oh my.

Twinkle, twinkle, little star.
How I wonder where you are.
Wish I may, wish I might,
Make this wish come true tonight.

Oh, ra ta ta ta tu.
Oh, ra ta ta ta tu.
Oh, ra ta ta oh.
There you are, little star.

Lollipop

Words and Music by Beverly Ross and Julius Dixon

recorded by The Chordettes

Refrain:
Lollipop, lollipop, oh, lolli, lolli, lolli,
Lollipop, lollipop, oh, lolli, lolli, lolli,
Lollipop, lollipop, oh, lolli, lolli, lolli, lollipop.

Call my baby lollipop, tell you why,
Her kiss is sweeter than an apple pie.
And when she does her shaky rockin' dance,
Man, I haven't got a chance. I call her

Refrain

Sweeter than candy on a stick,
Huckleberry, cherry, or lime;
If you had a choice, she'd be your pick,
But lollipop is mine. Oh.

Refrain

Crazy way she thrills-a me, tell you why,
Just like-a lightening from the sky.
She love to kiss me till I can't see straight,
Gee, my lollipop is great. I call her

Refrain

Lonely Boy

Words and Music by Paul Anka

recorded by Paul Anka

I'm just a lonely boy, lonely and blue;
I'm all alone with nothin' to do.
I've got ev'rything you could think of,
But all I want is someone to love.

Someone, yes, someone to love,
Someone to kiss, someone to hold at a moment like this.
I'd like to hear somebody say,
"I'll give you my love each night and day."

A lifetime of love means more to me
Than riches or fame untold.
Somewhere there's a someone waiting for me.
I'll find her before I grow too old.

Somebody, somebody, somebody, please send her to me
I'll make her happy, just wait and see.
I prayed so hard to the heavens above.
That I might find someone to love.

I'm just a lonely boy, lonely and blue;
I'm all alone with nothin' to do.
I've got ev'rything you could think of,
But all I want is someone to love.

Lonely Street

Words and Music by Carl Belew, W.S. Stevenson and Kenny Sowder

recorded by Andy Williams

Where's this place called lonely street?

I'm looking for that lonely street;
I've got a sad, sad tale to tell.
I need a place to go and weep.
Where's this place called lonely street?

A place where there's just loneliness;
Where dim lights bring forgetfulness.
Where broken dreams and mem'ries meet.
Where's this place called lonely street?

Perhaps upon that lonely street
There's someone such as I
Who came to bury broken dreams
And watch an old love die.

If I could find that lonely street
Where dim lights bring forgetfulness;
Where broken dreams and mem'ries meet.
Where's this place called lonely street?

Where's this place called lonely street?

Lonely Teardrops

Words and Music by Berry Gordy, Gwen Gordy Fuqua and Tyran Carlo

recorded by Jackie Wilson

Lonely teardrops, my pillow's never dry.
Lonely teardrops, come home, come home.
Just say you will, say you will, say you will.
Hey, hey, my heart is cryin', cryin'.

Lonely teardrops, my pillow's never dry.
Lonely teardrops, come home, come home.
Just say you will, say you will, say you will.
Hey, hey.

Just give me another chance for our romance.
Come on and tell me that one day you'll return,
'Cause ev'ry day that you've been gone away,
You'll know how my heart does nothing but burn.

Cryin' lonely teardrops, my pillow's never dry.
Lonely teardrops, come home, come home.
Just say you will, say you will, say you will.
Hey, hey, hey, say it right now, baby.
Come on, come on.

Lonesome Town

Words and Music by Baker Knight

recorded by Ricky Nelson

There's a place where lovers go
To cry their troubles away.
And they call it Lonesome Town,
Where the broken hearts stay.
(Lonesome Town.)

You can buy a dream or two
To last you all through the years.
And the only price you pay
Is a heart full of tears.
(Full of tears.)

Goin' down to Lonesome Town,
Where the broken hearts stay;
Goin' down to Lonesome Town,
To cry my troubles away.

In the town of broken dreams
The streets are paved with regret;
Maybe down in Lonesome Town
I can learn to forget. (To forget.)
Maybe down in Lonesome Town
I can learn to forget. (Lonesome Town.)

Love and Marriage

Words by Sammy Cahn
Music by James Van Heusen

a standard recorded by various artists

Love and marriage, love and marriage
Go together like a horse and carriage.
This I tell ya, brother,
Ya can't have one without the other.

Love and marriage, love and marriage,
It's an institute you can't disparage.
Ask the local gentry
And they will say it's elementary.

Try, try, try to separate them; it's an illusion.
Try, try, try and you will only come to this conclusion.

Love and marriage, love and marriage,
Go together like a horse and carriage.
Dad was told by Mother, you can't have one,
You can't have one without the other.

Love Me

Words and Music by Jerry Leiber and Mike Stoller

recorded by Elvis Presley

Treat me like a fool,
Treat me mean and cruel,
But love me.
Break my faithful heart,
Tear it all apart,
But love me.
If you ever go,
Darling, I'll be, oh, so lonely.
I'll be sad and blue,
Crying over you, dear, only.

I would beg and steal
Just to feel your heart
Beating close to mine.
Ev'ry night I pray
To the stars that shine
Above me,
Beggin' on my knees,
All I ask is please,
Please, love me.

Love Me Tender

Words and Music by Elvis Presley and Vera Matson

recorded by Elvis Presley

Love me tender, love me sweet;
Never let me go.
You have made my life complete,
And I love you so.

Refrain:
Love me tender, love me true
All my dreams fulfill.
For, my darlin', I love you,
And I always will.

Love me tender, love me long;
Take me to your heart.
For it's there that I belong,
And we'll never part.

Refrain

Love me tender, love me dear;
Tell me you are mine.
I'll be yours through all the years,
Till the end of time.

Refrain

A Lover's Question

Words and Music by Brook Benton and Jimmy Williams

recorded by Clyde McPhatter

Does she love me with all her heart?
Should I worry when we're apart?
A lover's questions I'd like to know
Oh, oh, oh, oh.

Does she need me as she pretends?
Is this a game? Will I win?
A lover's questions I'd like to know
Oh, oh, oh, oh.

I'd like to know when she's not with me
Is she still true to me?
I'd like to know when we're kissing
Does she feel just what I feel
And how am I to know it's really real?

Oh, tell me where the answer lies.
In her kiss or in her eyes?
A lover's questions I'd like to know
Oh, oh, oh, oh, oh.

Loving You

Words and Music by Jerry Leiber and Mike Stoller

recorded by Elvis Presley

I will spend my whole life through
Loving you, loving you.
Winter, summer, springtime, too,
Loving you, loving you.
Makes no diff'rence where I go or what I do.
You know that I'll always be loving you.

If I'm seen with someone new,
Don't be blue, don't be blue.
I'll be faithful, I'll be true,
Always true, true to you.
There is only one for me, and you know who.
You know that I'll always be loving you.

Magic Moments

Lyric by Hal David
Music by Burt Bacharach

recorded by Perry Como

I'll never forget the moment we kissed
The night of the hayride,
The way that we hugged to try to keep warm
While taking a sleigh ride.

Refrain:
Magic moments, mem'ries we've been sharing.
Magic moments, when two hearts are caring.
Time can't erase the mem'ry of these magic moments
Filled with love.

The telephone call that tied up the line
For hours and hours,
The Saturday dance I got up the nerve
To send you some flowers.

Refrain

The way that we cheered whenever our team
Was scoring a touchdown,
The time that the floor fell out of my car
When I put the clutch down.

Refrain

The penny arcade, the games that we played,
The fun and the prizes,
The Halloween Hop when ev'ryone came
In funny disguises.

Refrain

(You've Got) The Magic Touch

Words and Music by Buck Ram

recorded by The Platters

You've got the magic touch.
It makes me glow so much.
It casts a spell,
It rings a bell, the magic touch.

Oh, when I feel your charm,
It's like a four-alarm.
You make me thrill so much,
You've got the magic touch.

Here I go reeling,
Oh, oh I'm feeling the glow,
But where can I go from you?

I didn't know too much,
And then I felt your touch.
And now I learn
I can return the magic touch.

Maybe Baby

By Norman Petty and Charles Hardin

recorded by The Crickets

Maybe, baby, I'll have you.
Maybe, baby, you'll be true.
Maybe, baby, I'll have you for me.

It's funny, honey, you don't care.
You never listen to my prayer.
Maybe, baby, you will love me someday.

Well, you are the one that makes me sad,
And you are the one that makes me glad.
When someday you want me
I'll be there. Just wait and see.

Maybe, baby, I'll have you.
Maybe, baby, you'll be true.
Maybe, baby, I'll have you for me.

Memories Are Made of This

Words and Music by Richard Dehr, Frank Miller and Terry Gilkyson

recorded by Dean Martin, Gale Storm

Take one fresh and tender kiss.
Add one stolen night of bliss.
One girl, one boy:
Some grief, some joy.
Memories are made of this.

Don't forget a small moonbeam.
Fold in lightly with a dream.
Your lips and mine,
Two sips of wine.
Memories are made of this.

Then add the wedding bells,
One house where lovers dwell,
Three little kids for the flavor.
Stir carefully through the days;
See how the flavor stays,
These are the dreams you will savor.

With the blessings from above,
Serve it generously with love.
One man, one love, through life,
Memories are made of this.

Mister Sandman

Lyric and Music by Pat Ballard

recorded by The Chordettes

Boy:
Mister Sandman, bring me a dream,
Make her complexion like peaches and cream.
Give her two lips like roses in clover,
Then tell me that my lonesome nights are over.

Girl:
Mister Sandman, bring me a dream,
Make him the cutest that I've ever seen.
Give him the word that I'm not a rover,
Then tell me that my lonesome nights are over.

Refrain (both versions):
Sandman, I'm so alone;
Don't have nobody to call my own.
Please turn on your magic beam,
Mister Sandman, bring me a dream.

Mr. Wonderful

Words and Music by Jerry Bock, Larry Holofcener and George David Weiss

from the Musical *Mr. Wonderful*
recorded by Sarah Vaughan, Peggy Lee

Why this feeling?
Why this glow?
Why the thrill when you say, "Hello!"?
It's a strange and tender magic you do.
Mr. Wonderful,
That's you!

Why this trembling when you speak?
Why this joy when you touch my cheek?
I must tell you what my heart knows is true:
Mr. Wonderful,
That's you!

And why this longing to know your charms;
To spend forever here in your arms?
Oh! There's much more I could say,
But the words keep slipping away;
And I'm left with only one point of view:
Mr. Wonderful,
That's you!

One more thing, then I'm through;
Mr. Wonderful,
Mr. Wonderful,
Mr. Wonderful, I love you!

Misty

Words by Johnny Burke Music by Erroll Garner

a standard recorded by Johnny Mathis and various other artists

Look at me,
I'm as helpless as a kitten up a tree,
And I feel like I'm clinging to a cloud,
I can't understand,
I get misty just holding your hand.

Walk my way,
And a thousand violins begin to play,
Or it might be the sound of your hello,
That music I hear,
I get misty, the moment you're near.

You can say that you're leading me on,
But it's just what I want you to do,
Don't you notice how hopelessly I'm lost,
That's why I'm following you.

On my own,
Would I wander through this wonderland alone,
Never knowing my right foot from my left,
My hat from my glove,
I'm too misty and too much in love.

Moments to Remember

Words by Al Stillman
Music by Robert Allen

recorded by The Four Lads

The New Year's Eve we did the town,
The day we tore the goalpost down,
We will have these moments to remember.

The quiet walks, the noisy fun,
The ballroom prize we almost won,
We will have these moments to remember.

Though summer turns to winter
And the present disappears,
The laughter we were glad to share
Will echo through the years.

When other nights and other days
May find us gone our sep'rate ways,
We will have these moments to remember

Mona Lisa

Words and Music by Jay Livingston and Ray Evans

from the Paramount Picture *Captain Carey, U.S.A.*
a standard recorded by Nat "King" Cole and various other artists

In a villa in a little old Italian town
Lives a girl whose beauty shames the rose.
Many yearn to love her but their hopes all tumble down.
What does she want?
No one knows.

Refrain:
Mona Lisa, Mona Lisa men have named you.
You're so like the lady with the mystic smile.
Is it only 'cause you're lonely they have blamed you
For that Mona Lisa's strangeness in your smile?

Do you smile to tempt a lover, Mona Lisa,
Or is this your way to hide a broken heart?
Many dreams have been brought to your doorstep.
They just lie there, and they die there.
Are you warm, are you real, Mona Lisa,
Or just a cold and lonely, lovely work of art?

Refrain

Most of All

Words and Music by Alan Freed and Harvey Fuqua

recorded by The Moonglows

Most of all,
I want your warm embrace,
No one can take your place,
I need you most of all.

Most of all,
I want your sweet caress,
Truly, I must confess
I need you most of all.

When I sleep at night,
I dream wonderful, wonderful dreams of you;
And when I awake,
No one's there and that's why I'm so blue.

Most of all,
The one thing that I miss,
The way we used to kiss,
I need you most of all.

(Put Another Nickel In)
Music! Music! Music!

Words and Music by Stephan Weiss and Bernie Baum

recorded by Teresa Brewer

Put another nickel in, in the nickelodeon.
All I want is having you and music! Music! Music!
I'd do anything for you, anything you want me to.
All I want is kissing you and music! Music! Music!

Closer, my dear, come closer.
The nicest part of any melody
Is when you're dancing close to me.

So, put another nickel in, in the nickelodeon.
All I want is having you and music! Music! Music!
I'd do anything for you, anything you want me to.
All I want is kissing you and music! Music! Music!

My Heart Cries for You

Music by Percy Faith
Lyrics by Carl Sigman

a standard recorded by various artists

If you're in Arizona, I'll follow you.
If you're in Minnesota, I'll be there too.
You'll have a million chances to start anew,
Because my love is endless for you.

My heart cries for you,
Sighs for you, dies for you.
And my arms long for you.
Please come back to me.

The bloom has left the roses since you left me.
The birds have left my window since you left me.
I'm lonely as a sailboat that's lost at sea,
I'm lonely as a human can be.

My heart cries for you,
Sighs for you, dies for you.
And my arms long for you.
Please come back to me.

My Heart Is an Open Book

Lyric by Hal David
Music by Lee Pockriss

recorded by Carl Dobkins, Jr.

Refrain:
Look! Look! My heart is an open book.
I love nobody but you.
Look! Look! My heart is an open book.
My love is honest and true.

Some jealous so-and-so wants us to part.
That's why he's tellin' you that I've got a cheatin' heart.
Don't believe all those lies.
Darlin', just believe your eyes and
Look! Look! My heart is an open book.
I love nobody but you.

My Prayer

Music by Georges Boulanger
Lyric and Musical Adaptation by Jimmy Kennedy

recorded by The Platters

When the twilight is gone
And no song bird is singing;
When the twilight is gone
You come into my heart.
And here in my heart you will stay
While I pray.

My prayer is to linger with you,
At the end of the day,
In a dream that's divine.

My prayer is a rapture in blue,
With the world far away,
And your lips close to mine.

Tonight while our hearts are a-glow,
Oh! Tell me the words
That I'm longing to know.

My prayer and the answer you give,
May they still be the same,
For as long as we live;
That you'll always be there,
At the end of my prayer.

Never Be Anyone Else But You

Words and Music by Baker Knight

recorded by Ricky Nelson

There'll never be anyone else but you for me.
Never ever be, just couldn't be anyone else but you.

If I could take my pick of all the girls I've ever known.
Then I'd come and pick you out to be my very own.

There'll never be anyone else but you for me.
Never ever be, just couldn't be anyone else but you.

A heart that's true and longs for you is all I have to give.
All my love belongs to you as long as I may live.

There'll never be anyone else but you for me.
Never ever be, just couldn't be anyone else but you.

I never will forget the way you kiss me.
And when we're not together, I wonder if you miss me,
'Cause I hope and pray the day will come when you belong to me.
Then I'm gonna prove to you how true my love can be.

There'll never be anyone else but you for me.
Never ever be, just couldn't be anyone else but you.
Hmm, hmm.

No, Not Much!

Words by Al Stillman
Music by Robert Allen

recorded by The Four Lads

I don't want my arms around you no, not much!
I don't bless the day I found you no, not much!
I don't need you like the stars don't need the sky
I won't love you longer than the day I die.

You don't please me when you squeeze me no, not much!
My head's the lightest from your very slightest touch,
Baby, if you ever go, could I take it? Maybe so.
Ah, but would I like it? No, not much!

I don't care to hug and kiss you no, not much!
When you're gone I never miss you no, not much!
Like a ten cent soda doesn't cost a dime
I don't want you near me, only all the time.

You don't thrill me when you hold me no, not much!
My brain gets hazy from your cool and crazy touch,
Baby, if you ever go, could I take it? Maybe so.
Ah, but would I like it? No, not much! No, not much!

Oh Boy!

Words and Music by Sunny West, Bill Tilghman and Norman Petty

recorded by The Crickets

Refrain:
All of my love, all of my kissin',
You're gonna see what you been missin', oh boy!
When you're with me, oh boy!
The world can see that you were meant for me.

All of my life I been waitin',
Tonight there'll be no hesitatin', oh boy!
When you're with me, oh boy!
The world can see that you were meant for me.

Oh, can't you hear my poor heart callin',
Stars appear and shadows fall.
A little bit o' lovin' makes ev'rything right.
I'm gonna have some fun tonight!

Refrain

Oh! Carol

Words and Music by Howard Greenfield and Neil Sedaka

recorded by Neil Sedaka

Oh! Carol, I am but a fool.
Darling, I love you, though you treat me cruel.
You hurt me and you make me cry.
But if you leave me I will surely die.

Darling, there will never be another
'Cause I love you so.
Don't ever leave me. Say you'll never go.
I will always want you for my sweetheart,
No matter what you do.
Oh, oh, oh, Carol, I'm so in love with you.

Oh, Lonesome Me

Words and Music by Don Gibson

recorded by Don Gibson

Ev'rybody's goin' out and havin' fun.
I'm just a fool for stayin' home and havin' none.
I can't get over how she set me free.
Oh, lonesome me.

A bad mistake I'm makin' by just hangin' round.
I know that I should have some fun and paint the town.
A lovesick fool that's blind and just can't see.
Oh, lonesome me.

I'll bet she's not like me.
She's out and fancy free,
Flirting with the boys with all her charms.
But I still love her so,
And, brother, don't you know,
I'd welcome her right back here in my arms.

Well, there must be some way I can lose these lonesome blues.
Forget about the past and find somebody new.
I've thought of everything from A to Z.
Oh, lonesome me.

Oh! My Pa-Pa (O Mein Papa)

English Words by John Turner and Geoffrey Parsons
Music and Original Lyric by Paul Burkhard

a standard recorded by various artists

Oh! My Papa, to me he was so wonderful.
Oh! My Papa, to me he was so good.
No one could be so gentle and so lovable.
Oh! My Papa, he always understood.

Gone are the days
When he would take me on his knee
And with a smile
He'd change my tears to laughter.

Oh! My Papa, so funny, so adorable;
Always the clown, so funny in his way.
Oh! My Papa, to me he was so wonderful.
Deep in my heart I miss him so today.

Oh! My Papa. Oh! My Papa. Oh! My Papa.

Oh, Oh I'm Falling in Love Again

Words and Music by Dick Manning, Al Hoffman and Mark Markwell

recorded by Jimmie Rodgers

Many's the time I've been two-timed,
Many's the time I've been stung.
Many a honey took all of my money,
But that was when I was much younger.

Made up my mind to be careful,
Made up my mind to beware.
I was all right until Saturday night,
I met a gal with the goldenest hair.

Refrain:
Oh, oh, I'm falling in love again,
Oh, oh, oh, oh.
I thought I wouldn't get caught again.
Never in a hundred, never in a thousand,
Never in a million years!

She had the bluest of blue eyes,
She had the cheeriest lips.
Shouldn't-a kissed her, I tried to resist her,
But one kiss and I was a "goner."

I couldn't run if I wanted,
I couldn't run if I tried.
Saw what I liked and I liked what I saw,
And my heart went along for the ride.

Refrain

That was the end o' my rovin',
Now that it's over, I'm glad.
Through gallivantin', I got a new slantin',
I'm oh, oh, I'm a ring-a-ding daddy.

Rockin' a cradle at nighttime,
Livin' an' lovin' each day.
Got me a wife, she's the light o' my life,
An' when I kiss her good mornin', I say:

Refrain

Repeat and fade:
Never in a hundred, never in a thousand,
Never in a million years!

Old Cape Cod

Words and Music by Claire Rothrock, Milt Yakus and Allen Jeffrey

recorded by Patti Page

If you're fond of sand dunes and salty air,
Quaint little villages here and there;
You're sure to fall in love with old Cape Cod.

If you like the taste of a lobster stew,
Served by a window with an ocean view;
You're sure to fall in love with old Cape Cod.

Winding roads that seem to beckon you,
Miles of green beneath the skies of blue;
Church bells chiming on a Sunday morn',
Remind you of the town where you were born.

If you spend an evening, you'll want to stay,
Watching the moonlight on Cape Cod Bay;
You're sure to fall in love with old Cape Cod.

On the Street Where You Live

Words by Alan Jay Lerner Music by Frederick Loewe

from *My Fair Lady*
recorded by Vic Damone

I have often walked
Down this street before
But the pavement always stayed beneath my feet before.
All at once am I,
Several stories high,
Knowing I'm on the street where you live.

Are there lilac trees
In the heart of town?
Can you hear a lark in any other part of town?
Does enchantment pour
Out of every door?
No, it's just on the street where you live.

And oh, the towering feeling,
Just to know somehow you are near!
The overpowering feeling
That any second you may suddenly appear!

People stop and stare,
They don't bother me;
For there's nowhere else on earth that I would rather be.

Let the time go by,
I won't care if I
Can be here on the street where you live.

One Night

Words and Music by Dave Bartholomew and Pearl King

recorded by Elvis Presley

One night with you
Is what I'm now praying for.
The things that we two could plan
Would make my dreams come true.

Just call my name
And I'll be right by your side.
I want your sweet helping hand;
My love's too strong to hide.

Always lived a very quiet life.
I ain't never did no wrong.
Now I know that life without you
Has been too long.

One night with you
Is what I'm now praying for.
The things that we two could plan
Would make my dreams come true.

Only You (And You Alone)

Words and Music by Buck Ram and Ande Rand

recorded by The Platters

Only you
Can make this world seem right,
Only you
Can make the darkness bright.
Only you and you alone
Can thrill me like you do,
And fill my heart with love
For only you.

Only you
Can make this change in me
For it's true,
You are my destiny.
When you hold my hand,
I understand
The magic that you do.
You're my dream come true,
My one and only you.

Party Doll

Words and Music by James Bowen and Buddy Knox

recorded by Buddy Knox with The Rhythm Orchids

Well, all I want is a party doll
To come along with me when I'm feelin' wild,
To be ever lovin' and true and fair,
To run her fingers through my hair.

Refrain:
Come along and be my party doll.
Come along and be my party doll.
Come along and be my party doll.
I'll make love to you, to you,
I'll make love to you.

Well, I saw a gal walkin' down the street,
The kind of a gal I would love to meet.
She had blonde hair and eyes of blue.
Baby, I'm a-gonna have a party with you.

Refrain

Ev'ry man has gotta have a party doll,
To be with him when he's feelin' wild,
To be ever lovin', true, and fair,
To run her fingers through his hair,
To run her fingers through his hair.

Refrain

Peggy Sue

Words and Music by Jerry Allison, Norman Petty and Buddy Holly

recorded by Buddy Holly

If you knew Peggy Sue,
Then you'd know why I feel blue
About Peggy,
'Bout my Peggy Sue
Oh, well, I love you, gal,
Yes, I love you, Peggy Sue.

Peggy Sue, Peggy Sue,
Oh, how my heart yearns for you,
Oh, Pa-heggy,
My Pa-heggy Sue.
Oh, well, I love you, gal,
Yes, I love you, Peggy Sue.

Peggy Sue, Peggy Sue,
Pretty, pretty, pretty, pretty Peggy Sue,
Oh, my Peggy
My Peggy Sue
Oh, well, I love you gal,
And I need you, Peggy Sue.

I love you, Peggy Sue,
With a love so rare and true,
Oh, Peggy,
My Peggy Sue
Oh, well, I love you, gal
Yes, I want you,
Peggy Sue.

(You've Got) Personality

Words and Music by Lloyd Price and Harold Logan

recorded by Lloyd Price

Over and over, I tried to prove my love to you.
Over and over, what more can I do?
Over and over, my friends say I'm a fool.
But over and over, I'll be a fool for you.

Refrain:
'Cause you've got personality,
Walk, personality, talk, personality,
Smile, personality, charm personality,
Love personality,
And you've got a great big heart.
So, over and over, oh, I'll be a fool for you.
Now, over and over, what more can I do?

Over and over, I said that I loved you.
Over and over, honey, now it's the truth.
Over and over, they still say I'm a fool.
But over and over, I'll be a fool for you.

Refrain

Please Mr. Sun

Lyric by Sid Frank
Music by Ray Getzov

recorded by Tommy Edwards

Talk to him please, Mister Sun.
Speak to him, Mister Rainbow.
And take him under your branches, Mister Tree.

Whisper to him, Mister Wind.
Sing to him, Mister Robin.
And Missus Moonlight, put in a word for me.

Tell him how I feel;
It shouldn't end this way.
Since you are all his friends,
He'll listen to whatever you have to say.

Babble to him, Mister Brook.
Kiss him for me, Miss Raindrop.
And watch to see they all do, please Mister Sun.

Peter Cottontail

Words and Music by Steve Nelson and Jack Rollins

recorded by Gene Autry

Easter Version:
Here comes Peter Cottontail,
Hoppin' down the bunny trail,
Hippity hoppin', Easter's on its way.
Bringin' ev'ry girl and boy
Baskets full of Easter joy,
Things to make your Easter bright and gay.

He's got jelly beans for Tommy,
Colored eggs for sister Sue,
There's an orchid for your Mommy and an Easter bonnet, too.

Oh! Here comes Peter Cottontail,
Hoppin' down the bunny trail;
Hippity hoppity, Happy Easter day.

Here comes Peter Cottontail,
Hoppin' down the bunny trail;
Look at him stop, and listen to him say:
"Try to do the things you should."
Maybe if you're extra good,
He'll roll lots of Easter eggs your way.

You'll wake up on Easter morning
And you'll know that he was there
When you find those chocolate bunnies that he's hiding ev'rywhere.

Oh! Here comes Peter Cottontail,
Hoppin' down the bunny trail;
Hippity hoppity Happy Easter day.

Year-round Version:
Look at Peter Cottontail,
Hoppin' down the bunny trail,
A rabbit of distinction so they say.
He's the king of Bunny Land,
'Cause his eyes are shiny and
He can spot the wolf a mile away.

When the others go for clover
And the big bad wolf appears,
He's the one that's watching over givin' signals with his ears.

And that's why folks in Rabbit town
Feel so free when he's around
Peter's helpin' someone ev'ry day.

Little Peter Cottontail,
Hoppin' down the bunny trail,
Happened to stop for carrots on the way.
Something told him it was wrong,
Farmer Jones might come along
And an awful price he'd have to pay.

But he knew his legs were faster
So he nibbled three or four,
And he almost met disaster when he heard that shotgun roar.

Oh, that's how Peter Cottontail
Hoppin' down the bunny trail;
Lost his tail, but still he got away.

Poor Little Fool

Words and Music by Sharon Sheeley

recorded by Ricky Nelson

I used to play around with hearts that hastened at my call.
But when I met that little girl I knew that I would fall,
Poor little fool, oh yeah. I was a fool, uh-huh.
(Uh-huh, poor little fool. I was a fool, oh yeah.)

She'd play around and tease me with her carefree devil eyes.
She'd hold me close and kiss me, but her heart was full of lies,
Poor little fool, oh yeah. I was a fool, uh-huh.
(Uh-huh, poor little fool. I was a fool, oh yeah.)

She told me how she cared for me, that we'd never part.
And so for the very first time I gave away my heart,
Poor little fool, oh yeah. I was a fool, uh-huh.
(Uh-huh, poor little fool. I was a fool, oh yeah.)

The next day she was gone and I knew she lied to me.
She left me with a broken heart, won her victory,
Poor little fool, oh yeah. I was a fool, uh-huh.
(Uh-huh, poor little fool. I was a fool, oh yeah.)

Well, I've played this game with other hearts but
    I never thought I'd see
The day when someone else would play love's foolish game with me,
Poor little fool, oh yeah. I was a fool, uh-huh.
(Uh-huh, poor little fool. I was a fool, oh yeah, oh yeah.)

Primrose Lane

Words and Music by Wayne Shanklin and George Callender

recorded by Jerry Wallace

Primrose Lane,
Life's a holiday on Primrose Lane,
Just a holiday on Primrose Lane with you.

Can't explain,
When we're walkin' down Primrose Lane,
Even roses bloomin' in the rain with you.

Sweet perfume!
Those little ol' roses bloom
And I wanna walk with you my whole life through.

Primrose Lane,
Life's a holiday on Primrose Lane,
Just a holiday on Primrose Lane with you.

Problems

Words and Music by Boudleaux Bryant and Felice Bryant

recorded by The Everly Brothers

Problems, problems, problems all day long.
Will my problems work out right or wrong?
My baby don't like anything I do.
My teacher seems to feel the same way, too.

Worries, worries pile up on my head.
Woe is me; I should have stayed in bed.
Can't get the car; my marks ain't been so good.
My love life just ain't swingin' like it should.

Problems, problems, problems.
They're all on account of my lovin' you like I do.
Problems, problems, problems.
They won't be stopped until I'm sure of you.

You can solve my problems with a love that's true.
Problems, problems, problems all day long.

Repeat and fade:
Problems, problems, problems all day long.

Put Your Head on My Shoulder

Words and Music by Paul Anka

recorded by Paul Anka

Put your head on my shoulder,
Hold me in your arms, baby.
Squeeze me oh so tight, show me
That you love me too.

Put your lips close to mine, dear.
Won't you kiss me once, baby?
Just a kiss goodnight, maybe
You and I will fall in love.

People say that love's a game,
A game you just can't win.
If there's a way I'll find it someday,
And then this fool will rush in.

Put your head on my shoulder,
Whisper in my ear, baby,
Words I want to hear. Tell me,
Tell me that you love me too.

Put your head on my shoulder,
Whisper in my ear, baby,
Words I want to hear. Baby,
Put your head on my shoulder.

Que Sera, Sera
(Whatever Will Be, Will Be)

Words and Music by Jay Livingston and Ray Evans

from *The Man Who Knew Too Much*
recorded by Doris Day

When I was just a little girl
I asked my mother, "What will I be?
Will I be pretty? Will I be rich?"
Here's what she said to me:

Refrain:
"Que sera, sera,
Whatever will be will be.
The future's not ours to see.
Que sera, sera! What will be will be!"

When I was just a child in school,
I asked my teacher, "What should I try?
Should I paint pictures? Should I sing songs?"
This was her wise reply:

Refrain

When I grew up and fell in love,
I asked my lover, "What lies ahead?
Will we have rainbows day after day?"
Here's what my lover said:

Refrain

Now I have children of my own,
They ask their mother, "What will I be?
Will I be pretty? Will I be rich?"
I tell them tenderly:

Refrain

Que sera, sera!

Rag Mop

Words and Music by Johnnie Lee Wills and Deacon Anderson

a standard recorded by various artists

M, I say M-O, M-O-P,
M-O-P-P, Mop! M-O-P-P,
Mop! Mop! Mop! Mop!

R, I say R-A, R-A-G,
R-A-G-G, Rag! R-A-G-G,
M-O-P-P.

Rag Mop! Rag Mop!
Rag! Mop! Rag Mop! Rag Mop!
R-A-G-G, M-O-P-P, Rag Mop!

M, I say M-O, M-O-P,
M-O-P-P, Mop! M-O-P-P,
Mop! Mop! Mop! Mop!

R, I say R-A, R-A-G,
R-A-G-G, Rag! R-A-G-G,
M-O-P-P.

Rag Mop! Rag Mop!
Rag! Mop! Rag Mop! Rag Mop!
R-A-G-G, M-O-P-P, Rag Mop!

Return to Me

Words and Music by Danny Di Minno and Carmen Lombardo

recorded by Dean Martin

Return to me, oh, my dear, I'm so lonely;
Hurry back, hurry back, oh, my love, hurry back, I am yours.
Return to me, for my heart wants you only;
Hurry home, hurry home, won't you please hurry home to my heart.

My darling, if I hurt you, I'm sorry;
Forgive me, and please say you are mine!
Return to me, please come back, bella mia;
Hurry back, hurry home to my arms, to my lips, and my heart.

Italian lyrics:
Ritorna a me, non la sciare mi solo;
Vieni tu, vieni tu, vieni tu, vieni tu, mi amor.
Ritorna a me, cara mia ti amo;
Solo tu, solo tu, solo tu, solo tu, mio cuor.

Banbina, dar il couranes suno;
Mantieni, solamente per me.
Ritorna me, e la santa vemuta;
Vieni tu, vieni tu solo tu, solo tu me amor!

Rock and Roll Is Here to Stay

Words and Music by David White

recorded by Danny & The Juniors

Rock, rock, rock,
Oh baby, rock, rock, rock,
Oh baby, rock, rock, rock,
Oh baby, rock, rock, rock,
Oh baby.

Rock and roll is here to stay,
And it will never die.
It was meant to be that way,
Though I don't know why.
I don't care what people say,
Rock and roll is here to stay!
We don't care what people say,
Rock and roll is here to stay.

Rock and roll will always be,
I dig it to the end.
It'll go down in history,
Just you watch, my friend.
Rock and roll will always be,
It'll go down in history.
Rock and roll will always be,
It'll go down in history.

Ev'rybody rock, ev'rybody rock,
Ev'rybody rock, ev'rybody rock.
Come on, ev'rybody rock and roll.
Ev'rybody rock and roll.
Ev'rybody rock and roll.
Ev'rybody rock and roll.
Ev'rybody rock and roll.
Come on, ev'rybody rock and roll.

If you don't like rock and roll,
Just think what you've been missin',
But if you like to bop and stroll,
Walk around and listen.
Let's all start to rock and roll,
Ev'rybody rock and roll.
We don't care what people say,
Rock and roll is here to stay.

Rock and roll will always be,
I dig it to the end.
It'll go down in history,
Just you watch, my friend.
Rock and roll will always be,
It'll go down in history.
Rock and roll will always be,
It'll go down in history.

Rock Around the Clock

Words and Music by Max C. Freedman and Jimmy DeKnight

recorded by Bill Haley & His Comets

One, two, three o'clock, four o'clock, rock,
Five, six, seven o'clock, eight o'clock, rock,
Nine, ten, eleven o'clock, twelve o'clock, rock,
We're gonna rock around the clock tonight.

Put your glad rags on and join me, hon,
We'll have some fun when the clock strikes one.

Refrain:
We're gonna rock around the clock tonight.
We're gonna rock, rock, rock, 'til broad daylight.
We're gonna rock, gonna rock around the clock tonight.

When the clock strikes two, and three, and four,
If the band slows down we'll yell for more.

Refrain

When the chimes ring five, six, and seven,
We'll be rockin' up in seventh heav'n.

Refrain

When it's eight, nine, ten, eleven, too,
I'll be goin' strong and so will you.

Refrain

When the clock strike twelve, we'll cool off, then
Start a-rockin' 'round the clock again.

Refrain

Rockin' Robin

Words and Music by J. Thomas

recorded by Bobby Day

He rocks in the treetop, all the day long,
Hoppin' and a-boppin' and a-singin' his song.
All the little birds on Jaybird Street,
Love to hear the robin go "Tweet, tweet, tweet."

Refrain:
Rockin' Robin, Rockin' Robin,
Blow, Rockin' Robin,
'Cause we're really gonna rock tonight.

Ev'ry little swallow, ev'ry chickadee,
Ev'ry little bird in the tall oak tree.
The wise old owl, the big black crow,
Flap their wings, singin' "Go bird, go."

Refrain

A pretty little raven at the bird bandstand,
Taught him how to do the bop and it was grand.
They started goin' steady, and bless my soul,
He outbopped the buzzard and the oriole.

He rocks in the treetop, all the day long,
Hoppin' and a-boppin' and a-singin' his song.
All the little birds on Jaybird Street,
Love to hear the robin go "Tweet, tweet, tweet."

Refrain

A Rose and a Baby Ruth

Words and Music by John D. Loudermilk

recorded by George Hamilton IV

We had a quarrel, a teenage quarrel.
Now I'm as blue as I know how to be.
I can't see you at your home.
I can't even call you on the phone.
So I'm sending you this present
Just to prove I was telling the truth.

Dear, I believe you won't laugh when you receive
This rose and a Baby Ruth.
I could have sent you an orchid of some kind,
But that's all I had in my jeans at the time.
So I'm sending you this present,
And just to prove I was telling the truth,
I'll kiss you too, then I'll hand to you
A rose and a Baby Ruth.

Roving Kind

Words and Music by Jesse Cavanaugh and Arnold Stanton

recorded by Guy Mitchell, The Weavers

As I cruised one evening upon a night's career,
I spied a lofty clipper ship and to her I did steer.
I histed out my signals, which she so quickly knew
And when she saw my bunting fly she immediately hove to.

Refrain:
She had a dark and a roving eye,
And her hair hung down in ringalets.
She was a nice girl, a proper girl
But one of the roving kind.

"Oh, pardon me," she says to me, "For being out so late.
But if my parents heard of this, oh sad would be my fate.
My father is in politics, a good and righteous man.
My mother is an acrobat, and I do the best I can."

Refrain

I took her for some fish and chips and treated her so fine,
And hardly did I realize she was the roving kind.
I kissed her lips, I missed her lips, and found to my surprise,
She was nothing but a pirate ship rigged up in a disguise.

Refrain

So come all you good sailor men who sail the wint'ry sea,
And come all you apprentice lads, a warning take from me:
Bewared of lofty clipper ships, they'll be the ruin of you,
For t'was there she made me walk the plank and pushed me under too.

Refrain

Sea of Love

Words and Music by George Khoury and Philip Baptiste

recorded by Phil Phillips with The Twilights

Do you remember when we met?
That's the day I knew you were my pet.
I want to tell you
Just how much I love you.

Refrain:
Come with me my love
To the sea, the sea of love.
I want to tell you
Just how much I love you.

Come with me
To the sea
Of love.

Repeat Verse 1

Come with me
To the sea
Of love.

Refrain

I want to tell you,
Oh, how much
I love you.

Searchin'

Words and Music by Jerry Leiber and Mike Stoller

recorded by The Coasters

Gonna find her, gonna find her,
Gonna find her. Gonna find her.
Yes, I've been searchin', I've been searchin',
Oh, yeah, searchin' ev'ry which a-way, yeah, yeah.

Oh, yes, searchin', searchin',
searchin ev'ry which a-way, yeah, yeah.
But I'm like the Northwest Mountie
You know I'll bring her in some day.

Well, now if I have to swim a river, you know I will
And if I have to climb a mountain, you know I will.
And if she's hiding up on a blueberry hill,
Am I gonna find her, child, you know I will.

'Cause I've been searchin'. Oh, yeah, searchin'.
My goodness, searchin ev'ry which a-way, yeah, yeah.
But I'm like the Northwest Mountie
You know I'll bring her in some day.

Well, Sherlock Holmes, Sam Spade got nothing, child, on me.
Sargeant Friday, Charlie Chan and Boston Blackie,
No matter where she's hiding she's gonna hear me coming.
I'm gonna walk right down that street like Bulldog Drummond.

'Cause I've been searchin'. Oh, Lord, searchin'.
Um, child, searchin ev'ry which a-way, yeah, yeah.
But I'm like the Northwest Mountie
You know I'll bring her in some day. Gonna find her.

Secretly

Words and Music by Al Hoffman, Dick Manning and Mark Markwell

recorded by Jimmie Rodgers

Why must I meet you in a secret rendezvous?
Why must we steal away to steal a kiss or two?
Why must we wait to do the things we want to do?
Why, oh why, oh why, oh why, oh why?

Wish we didn't have to meet secretly.
Wish we didn't have to kiss secretly.
Wish we didn't have to be afraid
To show the world that we're in love!

Till we have the right to meet openly,
Till we have the right to kiss openly,
We'll just have to be content to be in love secretly!
Why, oh why, oh why, oh why, oh why?

See Saw

Words and Music by Steve Cropper and Don Covay

recorded by The Moonglows

Sometimes you love me like a good man ought-a;
Sometimes you hurt me so bad my tears run like water.
You get me out right before your friends,
Then you kiss on me, baby, until we're alone again.

Refrain:
Your love is like a seesaw,
Your love is like a seesaw, baby.
Your love is like a seesaw,
Goin' up, down, all around like a seesaw.

Sometimes you tell me you're gonna be my sweet candy man;
Then, uh, sometimes baby, don't know where I stand.
Lift me up when I'm on the ground,
But soon as I get up, you send me tumblin' down.

Refrain

When I kiss you, and I like it
And I ask you to kiss me again.
When I reach for you, you jump clean out of sight
You change just like the wind!

Repeat and fade:
Your love is like a seesaw,
Your love is like a seesaw, baby.

See You Later, Alligator

Words and Music by Robert Guidry

recorded by Bill Haley & His Comets

Well, I saw my baby walking, with another man today,
Well I saw my baby walking, with another man today,
When I asked her what's the matter, this is what I heard her say.

Refrain:
See you later, alligator, after 'while, crocodile;
See you later, alligator, after 'while, crocodile;
Can't you see you're in my way, now?
Don't you know you cramp my style?

When I thought of what she told me, nearly made me lose my head,
When I thought of what she told me, nearly made me lose my head.
But the next time that I saw her, reminded her of what she said.

Refrain

Shake, Rattle and Roll

Words and Music by Charles Calhoun

recorded by Bill Haley & His Comets

Get out from that kitchen and rattle those pots and pans.
Get out from that kitchen and rattle those pots and pans.
Well, roll my breakfast, 'cause I'm a hungry man.

Refrain:
Shake, rattle and roll.
Shake, rattle and roll.
Shake, rattle and roll.
Shake, rattle and roll.
You never do nothin' to save your doggone soul.

Wearin' those dresses, your hair done up so right.
Wearin' those dresses, your hair done up so right.
You look so warm, but your heart is cold as ice.

Refrain

I'm like a one-eyed cat, peepin' in a seafood store.
I'm like a one-eyed cat, peepin' in a seafood store.
I can look at you, tell you don't love me no more.

I believe you're doin' me wrong, and now I know.
I believe you're doin' me wrong, and now I know.
The more I work, the faster my money goes.

Refrain

Sh-Boom
(Life Could Be a Dream)

Words and Music by James Keyes, Claude Feaster, Carl Feaster,
Floyd McRae and James Edwards

recorded by The Crew-Cuts

Hey nonny ding dong, a-lang a-lang a-lang.
Boom ba-doh, ba-doo ba-doo.

Refrain:
Oh, life could be a dream,
(Sh-boom) If I could take you up in paradise up above.
(Sh-boom) If you would tell me I'm the only one that you love,
Life could be a dream, sweetheart.

(Hello, hello again, sh-boom, and hopin' we'll meet again.)

Oh, life could be a dream,
(Sh-boom) If only all my precious plans would come true.
(Sh-boom) If you would let me spend my whole life lovin' you,
Life could be a dream, sweetheart.

Ev'ry time I look at you,
Something is on my mind.
If you'd do what I want you to,
Baby, we'd be so fine.

Refrain

Twice:
Sh-boom sh-boom, ya-da-da da-da-da da-da-da-da
Sh-boom sh-boom, ya-da-da da-da-da da-da-da-da
Sh-boom sh-boom, ya-da-da da-da-da da-da-da-da, sh-boom.

Ev'ry time I look at you,
Something is on my mind.
If you'd do what I want you to,
Baby, we'd be so fine.

Refrain

Short Shorts

Words and Music by Bill Crandall, Tom Austin, Bob Gaudio and Bill Dalton

recorded by The Royal Teens

Boys:
Who wears short shorts?
Girls:
We wear short shorts.
Boys:
Bless 'em, short shorts.
Girls:
We like short shorts.
Boys:
Who wears short shorts?
Girls:
We wear short shorts.

Shrimp Boats

Words and Music by Paul Mason Howard and Paul Weston

recorded by Jo Stafford

Refrain:
Shrimp boats is a-comin', their sails are in sight.
Shrimp boats is a-comin', there's dancin' tonight.
Why don't-cha hurry, hurry, hurry home,
Why don't-cha hurry, hurry, hurry home?
Look, here the shrimp boats is a-comin',
There's dancin' tonight.

They go to sea with the evening tide
And their womenfolk wave their goodbye.
Ill sant vas, there they go.
While the Louisiana moon floats on high,
And they wait for the day they can cry.

Refrain

Happy the days while they're mending the nets
'Til once more they ride high out to sea.
Ill sant vas, there they go.
Then how lonely the long nights will be,
'Til that wonderful day when they see.

Refrain

Shout

Words and Music by O'Kelly Isley, Ronald Isley and Rudolph Isley

recorded by The Isley Brothers

Refrain:
You know you make me wanna
(Shout!) Kick my heels up and
(Shout!) Throw my hands up and
(Shout!) Throw my head back and
(Shout!) Come on, now.

Don't forget to say you will.
Don't forget to say yeah, yeah, yeah.
(Say you will.) Say it right now, baby.
(Say you will.) Well, come on, come on.
(Say you will.) Say that you.
(Say you will.)

(Say!) Say that you love me.
(Say!) Say that you need me.
Say that you want me.
Say you wanna please me.
(Say!) Come on now.
(Say!) Come on now.
(Say!) Come on now.
(Say!) I still remember
When I used to be nine years old, hey yeah.
And I was a fool for you
From the bottom of my soul.
Yeah, yeah, now that I found you,
I will never let you go, no, no.
And if you ever leave me.
You know it's gonna hurt me so.

I want you to know,
I said, I want you to know right now.
You been good to me, sisters,
Much better than I been to myself,
So good, so good.
And if you ever leave me,
I don't want nobody else, hey, hey.
I said, I want you to know, yeah,
I said, I want you to know right now.

Refrain

(Shout!) Come on now.
(Shout!) Come on now.
(Shout!) Come on now.
(Shout!) Play it, Sister Allen, hey.

Hey (hey), hey (hey),
Hey, yea, yea, yea. (Hey, yea, yea, yea.)
Hey, yea, yea, yea. (Hey, yea, yea.)

Repeat Ad Lib:
(Shout!) A little bit softer now.

Four Times:
(Shout!) A little bit louder now.

(Shout!) Get on up.
(Shout!) Get on up.
(Shout!)

Spoken:
All right now, come on, basses.
Bum, bum, bum, bum,
Bum, bum, bum, bum, bum.
Bum, bum, bum, bum,
Bum, bum, bum, bum, bum, bum.
Come on now.
Come on now.

Twice:
Shoo-be do-wop do wop, wop, wop, wop.
Shoo-be-do-be do-wop, do wop, wop, wop.

Shout, shout, shout, whoa.
Shout, shout, shout, whoa.
Hey (hey), hey (hey).

Refrain

Don't forget to say yeah,
Yeah, yeah, yeah, yeah.
Say you will.
Say you will.

Spoken:
Now wait a minute.
All right, who was that?
You know you make me wanna shout.

Silhouettes

Words and Music by Frank C. Slay Jr. and Bob Crewe

recorded by The Rays

Took a walk and passed your house late last night,
All the shades were pulled and drawn 'way down tight;
From within a dim light cast
Two silhouettes on the shade,
Oh, what a lovely couple they made.

Put his arms around your waist, held you tight,
Kisses I could almost taste in the night,
Wondered why I'm not the guy
Who's silhouette's on the shade
I couldn't hide the tears in my eyes.

Lost control, and rang your bell, I was sore,
"Let me in or else I'll beat down your door."
When two strangers, who had been
Two silhouettes on the shade
Said to my shock, "You're on the wrong block."

Rushed down to your house with wings on my feet,
Loved you like I've never loved you my sweet,
Vowed that you and I would be
Two silhouettes on the shade
All of our days,
Two silhouettes on the shade.

Since I Don't Have You

Words and Music by James Beaumont, Janet Vogel, Joseph Verscharen,
   Walter Lester, Lennie Martin, Joseph Rock and John Taylor

recorded by The Skyliners

I don't have plans and schemes
And I don't have daydreams.
I don't have anything
Since I don't have you.

I don't have fond desires
And I don't have happy hours.
I don't have anything
Since I don't have you.

I don't have happiness
And I guess I never will ever again.
When you walked out on me
In walked misery,
And he's been here since then.

Now I don't have much to share,
And I don't have one to care.
I don't have anything
Since I don't have you you you you
You you you you
You you you you
You.

Since I Met You Baby

Words and Music by Ivory Joe Hunter

recorded by Ivory Joe Hunter

Since I met you, baby, my whole life has changed.
Since I met you, baby, my whole life has changed
And ev'rybody tells me that I am not the same.

Refrain:
I don't need nobody to tell my troubles to.
I don't need nobody to tell my troubles to.
'Cause since I met you, baby, all I need is you.

Since I met you, baby, I'm a happy man.
Since I met you, baby, I'm a happy man.
I'm gonna try to please you in ev'ry way I can.

Refrain

Sincerely

Words and Music by Alan Freed and Harvey Fuqua

recorded by The McGuire Sisters

Sincerely, oh, yes, sincerely,
'Cause I love you so dearly.
Please say you'll be mine.
Sincerely, oh, you know how I love you.
I'll do anything for you;
Please say you'll be mine.

Oh, Lord, won't you tell me why I love that fella [girl] so?
He [she] doesn't want me.
Oh, I'll never, never, never, never let him [her] go.
Sincerely, oh, you know how I love you!
I'll do anything for you.
Please say you'll be mine.

Singing the Blues

Words and Music by Melvin Endsley

recorded by Guy Mitchell, Marty Robbins

Well, I never felt more like singing the blues
'Cause I never thought that I'd ever lose your love, dear.
Why'd you do me this way?

Well, I never felt more like crying all night
'Cause ev'rything's wrong and nothing ain't right without you.
You got me singing the blues.

The moon and stars no longer shine,
The dream is gone I thought was mine.
There's nothing left for me to do but cry over you.

Well, I never felt more like running away
But why should I go 'cause I couldn't stay without you.
You got me singing the blues.

(Seven Little Girls) Sitting in the Back Seat

Words by Bob Hilliard Music by Lee Pockriss

recorded by Paul Evans

Seven little girls sitting in the back seat,
Huggin' and a-kissin' with Fred.
I said, "Why don't one of you come up and sit beside me?"
And this is what the seven girls said:

Refrain:
All together now, one, two, three!
Keep your mind on your driving,
Keep your hands on the wheel.
Keep your snoopy eyes on the road ahead.
We're havin' fun sittin' in the back seat
Kissin' and a-huggin' with Fred.

Drove through the town, drove through the country,
Showed them how a motor could go.
I said, "How do you like my triple carburetor?"
And one of 'em whispered low:

Refrain

Seven little girls smoochin' in the back seat,
Ev'ry one in love with Fred.
I said, "You don't need me, I'll get off at my house."
And this is what the seven girls said:

Refrain

Sixteen Candles

Words and Music by Luther Dixon and Allyson R. Khent

recorded by The Crests

Sixteen candles make a lovely light,
But not as bright as your eyes tonight.
Blow out the candles, make your wish come true,
For I'll be wishing that you love me too.

You're only sixteen, but you're my teenage queen.
You're the prettiest, loveliest girl I've ever seen.
Sixteen candles in my heart will glow
For ever and ever, for I love you so.

So Long It's Been Good To Know Yuh (Dusty Old Dust)

Words and Music by Woody Guthrie

recorded by Woody Guthrie

I've sung this song but I'll sing it again,
Of the place that I lived on the wild, windy plains.
In the month called April, county called Gray,
And here's what all of the people there say:

Refrain:
So long, it's been good to know ya.
So long, it's been good to know ya.
So long, it's been good to know ya.
This dusty old dust is a gettin' my home,
And I've got to be driftin' along.

A dust storm hit, and it hit like thunder.
It dusted us over, and it covered us under.
Blocked out the traffic and blocked out the sun.
Straight for home all the people did run.

Refrain

We talked of the end of the world, and then
We'd sing a song and then sing it again.
We'd sit for an hour and not say a word,
And then these words would be heard:

Refrain

Sweethearts sat in the dark and sparked.
They hugged and kissed in that dusty old dark.
They sighed and cried, hugged and kissed.
Instead of marriage they talked like this:

Refrain

Now, the telephone rang and it jumped off the wall.
That was the preacher a makin' his call.
He said, "Kind friend, this may be the end,
And you've got your last chance at salvation of sin."

The churches was jammed, and the churches was packed,
And that dusty of dust storm blowed so black.
Preacher could not read a word of his text,
And he folded his specs, and he took up collection.

Refrain

Sound Off

By Willie Lee Duckworth and Bernard Lentz

recorded by Vaughn Monroe

Spoken: Hup! two, three, four. Hup! two, three, four.

Sung: The heads are up, the chests are out,
The arms are swingin', cadence count:
Sound off! (One two)
You mean sound off! (three four)
Cadence count: One, two, three, four.
One, two, three four!

Spoken: Hup! two, three, four. Hup! two, three, four.

Sung: Eeny, meeny, miney, mo,
Let's go back and count some more.
Sound off! (One two)
Let us sound off! (three, four)
Cadence count: One, two, three, four.
One, two, three four!

Oh, you had a good home but you left (You're right.)
And you wanna go home but you can't. (You're right.)
Now you think the gal that you left (You're right.)
Is waiting for you, but she ain't. (You're right.)

Now sound off! (One two)
Oh, you sound off! (three, four)
Cadence count: One, two, three, four.
One, two, three four!

Spoken: Hup! two, three, four. Hup! two, three, four.

Sung: Ain't no use in going home.
Alvin's got your gal and gone.
Ain't no use in feeling blue.
Alvin's got your sister too.

Now sound off! (One two)
Now you sound off! (three, four)
Cadence count: One, two, three, four.
One, two, three four!

Speedoo

Words and Music by Esther Navarro

recorded by The Cadillacs

Bom, bom, bom,
Bom, bom, bom,
Bom, bom, bom, bom.

Now they up and call me Speedoo,
But my real name is Mister Earl.
Now they up and call me Speedoo,
But my real name is Mister Earl.
All for meetin' brand-new fellows
And for takin' other folks' girls.

Now they up and call me Speedoo,
'Cause I don't believe in wastin' time.
Now they up and call me Speedoo,
'Cause I don't believe in wastin' time.
Now I've known some pretty women
And I thought that would change their minds.

Well, now, some they call me Joe.
Some they call me Moe.
Best man is Speedoo;
He don't never take it slow.

Now they up and call me Speedoo,
But my real name is Mister Earl.
Now they up and call me Speedoo,
But my real name is Mister Earl.
Now they're gonna call me Speedoo,
Till they call off makin' pretty girls.

Bom, bom, bom,
Bom, bom, bom,
Bom, bom, bom, bom.

Splish Splash

Words and Music by Bobby Darin and Murray Kaufman

recorded by Bobby Darin

Splish splash, I was taking a bath
Long about a Saturday night.
Rub-a-dub, just relaxing in the tub
Thinking everything was alright.
Well, I stepped out the tub, put my feet on the floor,
I wrapped the towel around me
And I opened the door, and then
Splish, splash! I jumped back in the bath.
Well, how was I to know there was a party going on?

They was a-splishin' and a-splashin',
Reelin' with the feelin',
movin' and a-groovin',
Rockin' and a-rollin', yeah!

Bing, bang, I saw the whole gang
Dancing on my living room rug, yeah!
Flip flop, they was doing the bop.
All the teens had the dancing bug.
There was Lollipop with-a Peggy Sue
Good Golly, Miss Molly was-a even there, too!
Ah, well-a, splish splash, I forgot about the bath.
I went and put my dancing shoes on, yeah.

I was a-rollin' and a-strollin',
Reeling with the feelin',
Moving and a-groovin',
Splishin' and a-splashin', yeah!

Yes, I was a-splishin' and a-splashin',
I was a-rollin' and a-strollin',
Yeah, I was a-movin' and a-groovin',
We was a-reeling with the feeling,
We was a-rollin' and a-strollin',
Movin' with the groovin',
Splish splash, yeah!

Splishin' and a-splashin',
I was a-splishin' and a-splashin',
I was a-movin' and a-groovin',
Yeah, I was a-splishin' and a-splashin'.

Sixteen Tons

Words and Music by Merle Travis

recorded by Tennessee Ernie Ford

Some people say a man is made out of mud
A poor man's made out of muscle and blood,
Muscle and blood and skin and bones,
A mind that's weak and back that's strong.

Refrain:
You load sixteen tons. What do you get?
Another day older and deeper in debt.
Saint Peter, don't you call me 'cause I can't go
I owe my soul to the company store.

I was born one mornin' when the sun didn't shine
I picked up my shovel and I walked to the mine,
I loaded sixteen tons of number nine coal.
And the straw boss said, "Well-a bless my soul."

Refrain

I was born one mornin', it was drizzling rain
Fightin' and trouble are my middle name.
I was raised in a cane brake by an ole mama lion.
Cain't no hightoned woman make me walk the line.

Refrain

If you see me comin' better step aside
A lotta men didn't, a lotta men died.
One first of iron, the other of steel.
If the right one don't-a get you, then the left one will.

Refrain

Stagger Lee

Words and Music by Lloyd Price and Harold Logan

recorded by Lloyd Price

The night was clear and the moon was yellow,
And the leaves came tumbling down.

I was standing on the corner when I heard my bulldog bark.
He was barking at the two men who were gambling in the dark.
It was Stagger Lee and Billy, two men who gamble late.
Stagger Lee threw seven, Billy swore that he threw eight.

Stagger Lee told Billy, "I can't let you go with that.
You have won all my money and my brand new Stetson hat."
Stagger Lee went home, and he got his forty-four.
Said, "I'm going to the barroom just to pay that debt I owe."

Stagger Lee went to the barroom, and he stood
    across the barroom door.
Said, "Now nobody move," and he pulled his forty-four.
"Stagger Lee," cried Billy, "oh please don't take my life.
I got three little children and a very sickly wife."

Stagger Lee shot Billy. Oh, he shot that poor boy so bad,
'Til the bullet come through Billy, and it broke the bartender's glass.
Go, Stagger Lee. Go, Stagger Lee. Go, Stagger Lee. Go, Stagger Lee.
Go, Stagger Lee. Go, Stagger Lee. Go, Stagger Lee. Go.

A Story Untold

Words and Music by Leroy Griffin

recorded by The Crew-Cuts

Well, here in my heart, there's a story untold
Of a girl who left me standing, standing in the cold.
And since she's been away, I've never had a happy day.
I hope and I pray that she'll hear my plea,
And maybe, someday, she'll come back to me.
For here in my heart, there's a story untold.

After all is said and done,
You said we'd be as one,
But darling, I found I was wrong.
And what did you do, right from the start?
You made a fool of me, and then you broke my heart.

I hope and I pray that she'll hear my plea,
And maybe, someday, she'll come back to me.
For here in my heart, there's a story untold.
Story, a story untold.

The Stroll

Words and Music by Clyde Otis and Nancy Lee

recorded by The Diamonds

Come, let's stroll, stroll across the floor.
Come, let's stroll, stroll across the floor.
Now turn around, baby, let's stroll once more.

I feel so good take me by the hand.
I feel so good take me by the hand,
And let's go strolling in wonderland.

Strolling,
Strolling, rock and rolling,
Strolling.

Well-a rock-a-my soul how I love to stroll.
There's my love strolling in the door.
There's my love strolling in the door.

Baby, let's go strolling by the candy store.

Stupid Cupid

Words and Music by Howard Greenfield and Neil Sedaka

recorded by Connie Francis

Stupid Cupid, you're a real mean guy.
I'd like to clip your wings so you can't fly.
I am in love and it's a cryin' shame,
And I know that you're the one to blame.
Hey, hey, set me free.
Stupid Cupid, stop pickin' on me.

I can't do my homework and I can't think straight.
I meet him ev'ry mornin' 'bout a half past eight.
I'm actin' like a lovesick fool.
You even got me carryin' his books to school.
Hey, hey, set me free.
Stupid Cupid, stop pickin' on me.

You mixed me up but good right from the very start.
Hey, go play Robin Hood with somebody else's heart.

You got me jumpin' like a crazy clown,
And I don't feature what you're puttin' down.
Since I kissed his lovin' lips of wine,
The thing that bothers me is that I like it fine.
Hey, hey, set me free.
Stupid Cupid, stop pickin' on me.

Sugartime

Words and Music by Charles Phillips and Odis Echols

recorded by The McGuire Sisters

Sugar in the mornin',
Sugar in the evenin',
Sugar at suppertime.
Be my little sugar
And love me all the time.

Honey in the mornin',
Honey in the evenin',
Honey at suppertime.
You'll be my little honey
And love me all the time.

Put your arms around me
And swear by the stars above,
You'll be mine forever
In a heaven of love.

Repeat Verse 1

Now sugar time is anytime
That you're near or just appear.
So don't you roam,
Just be my honeycomb.
We'll live in a heaven of love.

Repeat All Except Last Verse

Summertime, Summertime

Words and Music by Tom Jameson and Sherm Feller

recorded by The Jamies

It's summertime, summertime, sum-sum-summertime.
Summertime, summertime, sum-sum-summertime.
Summertime, summertime, sum-sum-summertime.
Summertime, summertime, sum-sum-summertime,
Summertime.

Well, shut them books and throw 'em away.
Say goodbye to dull school days.
Look alive and change your ways.
It's summertime.

Well, no more studying history,
And no more reading geography.
And no more dull geometry,
Because it's summertime.

Refrain:
It's time to head straight for them hills.
It's time to live and have some thrills.
Come along and have a ball,
A regular free for all.

Well, are you comin' or are you ain't?
You slowpokes are my one complaint.
Hurry up before I faint.
It's summertime.

Well, I'm so happy that I could flip;
Oh, how I love to take a trip.
I'm so sorry, teacher, but zip your lip,
Because it's summertime.

Refrain

Well, we'll go swimmin' ev'ry day.
No time to work, just time to play.
If your folks complain just say:
It's summertime.

And ev'ry night we'll have a dance,
'Cause what's a vacation without romance.
Oh, man, this jive has me in a trance,
Because it's summertime.

Refrain

It's summertime.

Sway (Quien Sera)

English Words by Norman Gimbel
Spanish Words and Music by Pablo Beltran Ruiz

a standard recorded by Dean Martin and other artists

When marimba rhythms start to play,
Dance with me, make me sway.
Like the lazy ocean hugs the shore,
Hold me close, sway me more.

Like a flower bending in the breeze,
Bend with me, sway with ease.
When we dance you have a way with me,
Stay with me, sway with me.

Other dancers may be on the floor,
Dear, but my eyes will see only you.
Only you have that magic technique,
When we sway I grow weak.

I can hear the sound of violins
Long before it begins.
Make me thrill as only you know how,
Sway me smooth, sway me now.

Quien sera la que me quieraa mi
Quien sera Quein sera
Quien sera la que me de su amor
Quien sera Quien sera.

Yo no se la po dre encontrar
Yo no se, you no se
You no se si volvere a querer
You no se, you no se

He querido volver a vivir
Las passion y el calor de otro amor
De otr amor que me hiciera sentir
Que me hiciera feliz

Como a yer lo fui quien sera la que me quiera a mi
Quien sera, quien sera
Quien sera la que me de su amor
Quien sera, quien sera, quien sera, quien sera.

Susie-Q

Words and Music by Dale Hawkins, Stan Lewis and Eleanor Broadwater

recorded by Dale Hawkins

Oh, Susie-Q, oh, Susie-Q
Oh Susie-Q, how I love you,
My Susie-Q.

I like the way you walk,
I like the way you talk;
I like the way you walk,
I like the way you talk, my Susie-Q

Oh, Susie-Q, oh, Susie-Q
Oh Susie-Q, how I love you,
My Susie-Q.

Well, say that you'll be true,
Well, say that you'll be true;
Well, say that you'll be true
And never leave me blue, my Susie-Q.

Tammy

Words and Music by Jay Livingston and Ray Evans

from *Tammy and the Bachelor*
recorded by Debbie Reynolds, The Ames Brothers

I hear the cottonwoods whisp'rin' above:
Tammy! Tammy! Tammy's my love!
The ole hootie owl hootie-hoos to the dove:
Tammy! Tammy! Tammy's my love!

Does my darling feel what I feel; when she comes near?
My heart beats so joyfully, you'd think she could hear!
Wish I knew if she knew what I'm dreaming of!
Tammy! Tammy! Tammy's my love!

Whippoorwill, whippoorwill, you and I know,
Tammy! Tammy! Can't let him go!
The breeze from the bayou keeps murmuring low:
Tammy! Tammy! You love him so!

When the night is warm, soft and warm, I long for his charms!
I'd sing like a violin if I were in his arms!
Wish I knew if he knew what I'm dreaming of!
Tammy! Tammy! Tammy's in love!

Teach Me Tonight

Words by Sammy Cahn
Music by Gene DePaul

a standard recorded by various artists

Did you say, "I've got a lot to learn?"
Well, don't think I'm trying not to learn.
Since this is the perfect spot to learn,
Teach me tonight.

Starting with the "A, B, C" of it,
Right down to the "X, Y, Z" of it,
Help me solve the mystery of it;
Teach me tonight.

The sky's a blackboard high above you.
If a shooting star goes by,
I'll use that star to write "I love you"
A thousand times across the sky.

One thing isn't very clear, my love.
Should the teacher stand so near, my love?
Graduation's almost here, my love.
Teach me tonight.

Tears on My Pillow

Words and Music by Sylvester Bradford and Al Lewis

recorded by Little Anthony & The Imperials

You don't remember me,
But I remember you.
'Twas not so long ago
You broke my heart in two.
Tears on my pillow, pain in my heart,
Caused by you.

If we could start anew,
I wouldn't hesitate.
I'd gladly take you back
And tempt the hand of fate.
Tears on my pillow, pain in my heart,
Caused by you.

Love is not a gadget, love is not a toy.
When you find the one you love
She'll fill your heart with joy.

Before you go away,
My darling, think of me.
There may be still a chance
To end my misery.
Tears on my pillow, pain in my heart,
Caused by you.

(Let Me Be Your) Teddy Bear

Words and Music by Kal Mann and Bernie Lowe

recorded by Elvis Presley

Baby, let me be your lovin' teddy bear.
Put a chain around my neck
And lead me anywhere.
Oh, let me be your teddy bear.

I don't want to be your tiger
'Cause tigers play too rough.
I don't want to be your lion
'Cause lions ain't the kind you love enough.

Refrain:
Just wanna be your teddy bear.
Put a chain around my neck
And lead me anywhere.
Oh, let me be your teddy bear.

Baby, let me be around you ev'ry night.
Run your fingers through my hair
And cuddle me real tight.
Oh, let me be your teddy bear.

I don't want to be your tiger
'Cause tigers play too rough.
I don't want to be your lion
'Cause lions ain't the kind you love enough.

Refrain

A Teenager in Love

Words and Music by Doc Pomus and Mort Shuman

recorded by Dion & The Belmonts

Each time we have a quarrel, it almost breaks a heart,
'Cause I'm so afraid that we will have to part.
Each night I ask the stars up above.
Why must I be a teenager in love?

One day I feel so happy, next day I feel so sad.
I guess I'll learn to take the good with the bad.
Each night I ask the stars up above,
Why must I be a teenager in love?

I cried a tear for nobody but you.
I'll be a lonely one if you should say we're through.

If you want to make me cry, that won't be so hard to do.
And if you should say goodbye, I'll still go on loving you.
Each night I ask the stars up above,
Why must I be a teenager in love?

Tennessee Waltz

Words and Music by Redd Stewart and Pee Wee King

recorded by Patti Page, Pee Wee King and various other artists

I was waltzing with my darlin'
To the Tennessee waltz,
When an old friend I happened to see.

Introduced him to my loved one
And while they were waltzing,
My friend stole my sweetheart from me.

I remember the night and the Tennessee Waltz.
Now I know just how much I have lost.
Yes, I lost my little darlin' the night they were playing
The beautiful Tennessee Waltz.

That'll Be the Day

Words and Music by Jerry Allison, Norman Petty and Buddy Holly

recorded by The Crickets

Well, you give me all your lovin'
And your turtle-dovin',
All your hugs an' your money too;
Well, you know you love me, baby,
Until you tell me, maybe, that someday, well,
I'll be through! Well,

Refrain:
That'll be the day,
When you say goodbye,
Yes, that'll be the day,
When you make me cry,
Ah, you say you're gonna leave,
You know it's a lie,
'Cause that'll be the day, when I die.

Well, when Cupid shot his dart,
He shot it at your heart,
So if we ever part and I leave you,
You say you told me an' you
Told me boldly, that some day, well,
I'll be through. Well,

Refrain

That's Amoré (That's Love)

Words by Jack Brooks
Music by Harry Warren

from the Paramount Picture *The Caddy*
a standard recorded by various artists

In Napoli, where love is king,
When boy meets girl, here's what they sing:

When the moon hits your eye
Like a big pizza pie,
That's amoré.
When the world seems to shine
Like you've had too much wine,
That's amoré.
Bells will ring, ting-a-ling-a-ling,
Ting-a-ling-a-ling, and you sing,
"Veeta bella."
Hearts will play, tippy-tippy-tay,
Tippy-tippy-tay like a gay tarantella.
(Lucky fella)

When the stars make you drool
Just like pasta fazool,
That's amoré.
When you dance down the street
With a cloud at you feet,
You're in love.
When you walk in a dream
But you know you're not dreaming,
Signoré.
Scuza me, but you see,
Back in old Napoli,
That's amoré.

There Goes My Baby

Words and Music by Jerry Leiber, Mike Stoller, Ben E. Nelson,
  Lover Patterson and George Treadwell

recorded by The Drifters

There goes my baby,
Movin' on down the line.
Wonderin' where, wonderin' where,
Wonderin' where she is bound.
I broke her heart and made her cry.
Now I'm alone, so all alone.
What can I do, what can I do?

(There goes my baby.
There goes my baby.
There she goes.)

Yes, I wanna know.
Did she love me?
Did she really love me?
Was she just playing me for a fool?
I wonder why she left me.
Why did she leave me
So all alone, so all alone?

I was gonna tell her that I love her
And that I need her
Beside my side to be my guide.
I wanna know where is my,
Where is my baby?
I want my baby.
I need my baby, yes.
Oh, oh, oh.

The Three Bells

Words and Music by Bert Reisfeld and Jean Villard

recorded by The Browns

There's a village hidden deep in the valley,
Among the pine trees half forlorn.
And there, on a sunny morning,
Little Jimmy Brown was born.

So his parents brought him to the chapel
When he was only one day old.
And the priest blessed the little fellow,
"Welcome, Jimmy, to the fold."

All the chapel bells were ringing
In the little valley town.
And the songs that they were singing
Was for baby Jimmy Brown.

Then the little congregation
Prayed for guidance from above,
"Lead us not into temptation.
Bless this hour of meditation.
Guide him with eternal love."

There's a village hidden deep in the valley,
Beneath the mountains high above.
And there, twenty years thereafter,
Jimmy was to meet his love.

Many friends were gathered in the chapel
And many tears of joy were shed
In June on a Sunday morning,
When Jimmy and his bride were wed.

All the chapel bells were ringing.
'Twas a great day in his life,
'Cause the songs that they were singing
Was for Jimmy and his wife.

Then the little congregation
Prayed for guidance from above,
"Lead us not into temptation.
Bless, O Lord, this celebration.
May their lives be filled with love."

From the village hidden deep in the valley,
One rainy morning dark and gray,
A soul winged its way to heaven,
Jimmy Brown had passed away.

Silent people gathered in the chapel
To say farewell to their old friend.
Whose life had been like a flower,
Budding, blooming to the end.

Just a lonely bell was ringing
In the little valley town.
'Twas farewell that it was singing
To our good old Jimmy Brown.

And the little congregation
Prayed for guidance from above,
"Lead us not into temptation.
May his soul find the salvation
Of Thy great eternal love."

Tom Dooley

Words and Music Collected, Adapted and Arranged by Frank Warner,
  John A. Lomax and Alan Lomax
From the singing of Frank Proffitt

recorded by The Kingston Trio

Refrain:
Hang down you head, Tom Dooley,
Hang down you head and cry,
Hand down your head, Tom Dooley,
Poor boy, you're bound to die.

I met her on the mountain,
And there I took her life,
I met her on the mountain
And stabbed her with my knife.

Refrain

This time tomorrow,
Reckon where I'll be?
If it had'n-a been for Grayson
I'd-a been in Tennessee.

Refrain

This time tomorrow,
Reckon where I'll be?
In some lonesome valley
A-hangin' on a white oak tree.

Refrain

Tonight You Belong to Me

Words by Billy Rose
Music by Lee David

recorded by Patience & Prudence

Though you belong to somebody else,
Tonight you belong to me.
Though we're apart, you're part of my heart,
Tonight you belong to me.

Down by the stream, how sweet it will seem,
Once more to dream in the moonlight.
Though with the dawn, I know you'll be gone,
Tonight you belong to me.

Too Much

Words and Music by Lee Rosenberg and Bernie Weinman

recorded by Elvis Presley

Honey, I love you too much.
Need your lovin' too much.
Want the thrill of your touch.
Gee, I can't hold you too much.
You do all the livin' while I do all the givin'
'Cause I love you too much.

You spend all my money too much.
Have to share you, honey, too much.
When I want some lovin', you're gone.
Don't you know you're treatin' me wrong.
Now you got me started, don't you leave me brokenhearted,
'Cause I love you too much.

Refrain:
Need your lovin' all the time,
Need your huggin'; please be mine.
Need you near me; stay real close.
Please, please hear me, you're the most.
Now you got me started, don't you leave me brokenhearted,
'Cause I love you too much.

Ev'ry time I kiss your sweet lips,
I can feel my heart go flip flip.
I'm such a fool for your charms,
Take me back, my baby, in your arms.
Like to hear you sighin' even though I know you're lyin',
'Cause I love you too much.

Refrain

Too Young

Words by Sylvia Dee
Music by Sid Lippman

a standard recorded by various artists

They try to tell us we're too young,
Too young to really be in love.
They say that love's a word,
A word we've only heard
But can't begin to know the meaning of.
And yet, we're not too young to know
This love will last though years may go.
And then, someday they may recall
We were not too young at all.

True Love

Words and Music by Cole Porter

from the film *High Society*
recorded by Bing Crosby & Grace Kelly, and various other artists

Suntanned, windblown
Honeymooners at last alone,
Feeling far above par,
Oh, how lucky we are
While—

I give to you and you give to me
True love, true love.
So, on and on it will always be
True love, true love.
For you and I
Have a guardian angel on high
With nothing to do
But to give to you and to give to me
Love, forever true.

Turn Me Loose

Words and Music by Doc Pomus and Mort Shuman

recorded by Fabian

Turn me loose, turn me loose, I say.
This is the first time I ever felt this way.
Gonna get a thousand kicks, gonna kiss a thousand chicks.
So turn me loose.

Turn me loose, turn me loose, I say.
Gonna rock and roll long as the band's gonna play.
Gonna holler, gonna shout, gonna knock myself right out,
So turn me loose.

I've got some change in my pocket and I'm rarin' to go.
I'm takin' some chick to the picture show.
When I see her home and we kiss goodnight,
Turn me loose, turn me loose, turn me loose, turn me loose.

Turn me loose, turn me loose, I say.
Yes, today is gonna be the day.
I want you all to understand that now I am a man,
So turn me loose.

26 Miles (Santa Catalina)

Words and Music by Glen Larson and Bruce Belland

recorded by The Four Preps

Twenty-six miles across the sea,
Santa Catalina is a-waitin' for me.
Santa Catalina, the island of romance,
Romance, romance, romance.
Water all around it ev'rywhere,
Tropical trees and the salty air;
But for me the thing that's a-waitin' there's romance.

It seems so distant, twenty-six miles away,
Restin' in the water serene.
I'd work for anyone, even the Navy,
Who would float me to my island dream.
Twenty-six miles, so near yet far.
I'd swim with just some water wings and my guitar.
I can leave the wings but I'll need the guitar for romance,
Romance, romance, romance.

Twenty-six miles across the sea,
Santa Catalina is a-waitin' for me.
Santa Catalina, the island of romance.

A tropical heaven out in the ocean
Covered with trees and girls.
If I have to swim, I'd do it forever
Till I'm gazin' on those island pearls.
Forty kilometers in a leaky old boat,
Any old thing that'll stay afloat.
When we arrive we'll all promote romance,
Romance, romance, romance.

Unchained Melody

Lyric by Hy Zaret
Music by Alex North

from the film *Unchained*
recorded by Les Baxter, Al Hibbler

Oh, my love, my darling,
I've hungered for your touch,
A long, lonely time.
Time goes by so slowly
And time can do so much,
Are you still mine?
I need your love, I need your love,
God speed your love to me!

Lonely rivers flow to the sea,
To the sea,
To the open arms
Of the sea.

Lonely rivers sigh,
"Wait for me,
Wait for me!"
I'll be coming home,
Wait for me.

Repeat Verse

Venus

Words and Music by Edward Marshall

recorded by Frankie Avalon

Hey, Venus, oh, Venus.
Hey, Venus, oh, Venus.

Venus, if you will,
Please send a little girl for me to thrill,
A girl who wants my kisses and my arms,
A girl with all the charms of you.

Venus, make her fair,
A lovely girl with sunlight in her hair,
And take the brightest stars up in the skies
And place them in her eyes for me.

Venus, goddess of love that you are,
Surely the things I ask can't be to great a task.

Venus, if you do,
I promise that I always will be true;
I'll give her all the love I have to give
As long as we both shall live.

Hey, Venus, oh, Venus.
Make my wish come true.
Hey, Venus, oh, Venus.
Hey, Venus, oh, Venus.

Wake Up Little Susie

Words and Music by Boudleaux Bryant and Felice Bryant

recorded by The Everly Brothers

Wake up, little Susie, wake up.
Wake up, little Susie, wake up.

We've both been sound asleep,
Wake up, little Susie, and weep.
The movie's over, it's four o'clock
And we're in trouble deep.

Refrain:
Wake up, little Susie, wake up, little Susie,
Well, what are we gonna tell your mama?
What are we gonna tell your pa?
What are we gonna tell our friends when they say,
"Ooh la la"
Wake up, little Susie, wake up, little Susie.

Well, we told your Mama that we'd be in by ten.
Well, Susie baby, looks like we goofed again
Wake up, little Susie, wake up, little Susie,
We've gotta go home.

Wake up, little Susie, wake up.
Wake up, little Susie, wake up.

The movie wasn't so hot,
It didn't have much of a plot.
We fell asleep, and our goose is cooked,
Our reputation is shot.

Refrain

Walkin' After Midnight

Lyrics by Don Hecht
Music by Alan W. Block

recorded by Patsy Cline

I go out walkin' after midnight
In the moonlight, just like we used to do.
I'm always walkin' after midnight searchin' for you.

I'll walk for miles along the highway,
That's just my way of being close to you.
I go out walkin' after midnight searchin' for you.

I stop to see a weepin' willow,
Cryin' on his pillow,
Maybe he's cryin' for me.
And as the sky turns gloomy,
Night winds whisper to me.
I'm lonely as lonely can be.

I'll go out walkin' after midnight
In the starlight and pray that you may be
Somewhere just walkin' after midnight searchin' for me.

Waterloo

Words and Music by John Loudermilk and Marijohn Wilkins

recorded by Stonewall Jackson

Now old Adam was the first in history
With an apple he was tempted and deceived.
Just for spite, the devil made him take a bite.
And that's where old Adam met his Waterloo.

Refrain:
Waterloo, Waterloo;
Where will you meet your Waterloo?
Ev'ry puppy has its day, ev'rybody has to pay.
Ev'rybody has to meet his Waterloo.

Little Gen'ral Napoleon of France
Tried to conquer the world, but lost his chance.
Met defeat, known as Bonaparte's retreat.
And that's where Napoleon met his Waterloo.

Refrain

Now a fellah whose darlin' proved untrue
Took her life, but he lost his too.
Now he swings where the little birdies sing,
And that's where Tom Dooley met his Waterloo.

Refrain

The Wayward Wind

Words and Music by Herb Newman and Stan Lebowsky

recorded by Gogi Grant

Refrain:
Oh, the wayward wind is a restless wind,
A restless wind that yearns to wander;
And he was born the next of kin, the next of kin
To the wayward wind.

In a lonely shack by a railroad track
He spent his younger days,
And I guess the sound of the outward bound
Made him a slave to his wand'rin' ways.

Refrain

Oh I met him there in a border town,
He vowed we'd never part,
Though he tried his best to settle down
I'm now alone with a broken heart.

Refrain

Wear My Ring Around Your Neck

Words and Music by Bert Carroll and Russell Moody

recorded by Elvis Presley

Won't you wear my ring up around your neck
To tell the world I'm yours, by heck.
Let them see your love for me,
And let them see by the ring around your neck.

Won't you wear my ring up around your neck
To tell the world I'm yours, by heck.
Let them know I love you so,
And let them know by the ring around your neck.

They say that going steady is not the proper thing.
They say that we're too young to know the meaning of a ring.
I only know I love you and that you love me too.
So, darling, please do what I ask of you.

Won't you wear my ring up around your neck
To tell the world I'm yours, by heck.
Let them see your love for me,
And let them see by the ring around your neck.

Won't you wear my ring up around your neck
To tell the world I'm yours, by heck.
Let them know I love you so,
And let them know by the ring around your neck.

Wheel of Fortune

Words and Music by Bennie Benjamin and George Weiss

recorded by Kay Starr

The wheel of fortune goes spinning around;
Will the arrow point my way? Will this be the day?
Oh! Wheel of fortune, please don't pass me by;
Let me know the magic of a kiss and a sigh.

While the wheel is spinning, spinning, spinning,
I'll not dream of winning fortune or fame;
While the wheel is turning, turning, turning,
I'll be ever yearning for love's precious flame!

Oh! Wheel of fortune, I'm hoping somehow
If you'll ever smile on me please let it be now.

A White Sport Coat (And a Pink Carnation)

Words and Music by Marty Robbins

recorded by Marty Robbins

A white sport coat and a pink carnation,
I'm all dressed up for the dance.
A white sport coat and a pink carnation,
I'm all alone in romance.

Once you told me long ago
To the Prom with me you'd go.
Now you've changed your mind, it seems
Someone else will hold my dreams.

A white sport coat and a pink carnation,
I'm all in a blue, blue mood.

Why

Words and Music by Bob Marcucci and Peter DeAngelis

recorded by Frankie Avalon

I'll never let you go, why, because I love you.
I'll always love you so, why, because you love me.
No broken hearts for us, 'cause we love each other.
And with our faith and trust, there could be no other.

Why, 'cause I love you, why, 'cause you love me.

I think you're awf'ly sweet, why, because I love you.
You say I'm your special treat, why, because you love me.
We found a perfect love, yes, a love that's yours and mine.
I love you and you love me all the time.

Why Do Fools Fall in Love

Words and Music by Morris Levy and Frankie Lymon

recorded by Frankie Lymon & The Teenagers

Oo-wah, oo-wah,
Oo-wah, oo-wah,
Oo-wah, oo-wah.
Why do fools fall in love?

Why do birds sing so gay
And lovers await the break of day?
Why do they fall in love?
Why does the rain fall from up above?
Why do fools fall in love?
Why do they fall in love?

Love is a losing game.
Love can be a shame.
I know of a fool, you see,
For that fool is me.
Tell me why.
Tell me why.

Why do birds sing so gay
And lovers await the break of day?
Why do they fall in love?
Why does the rain fall from up above?
Why do fools fall in love?
Why do they fall in love?

Why does my heart skip a crazy beat?
For I know it will reach defeat.
Tell me why,
Tell me why,
Why do fools fall in love?

Why Don't You Believe Me

Words and Music by Lew Douglas, Luther King Laney and Leroy W. Rodde

a standard recorded by various artists

Why don't you believe me
It's you I adore
Forever and ever
Can I promise more?

I've told you so often
The way that I care
Why don't you believe me
It just isn't fair.

Here is a heart that is lonely
Here is a heart you can take.
Here is a heart for you only,
That you can keep or break.

How else can I tell you
What more can I do
Why don't you believe me?
I love only you.